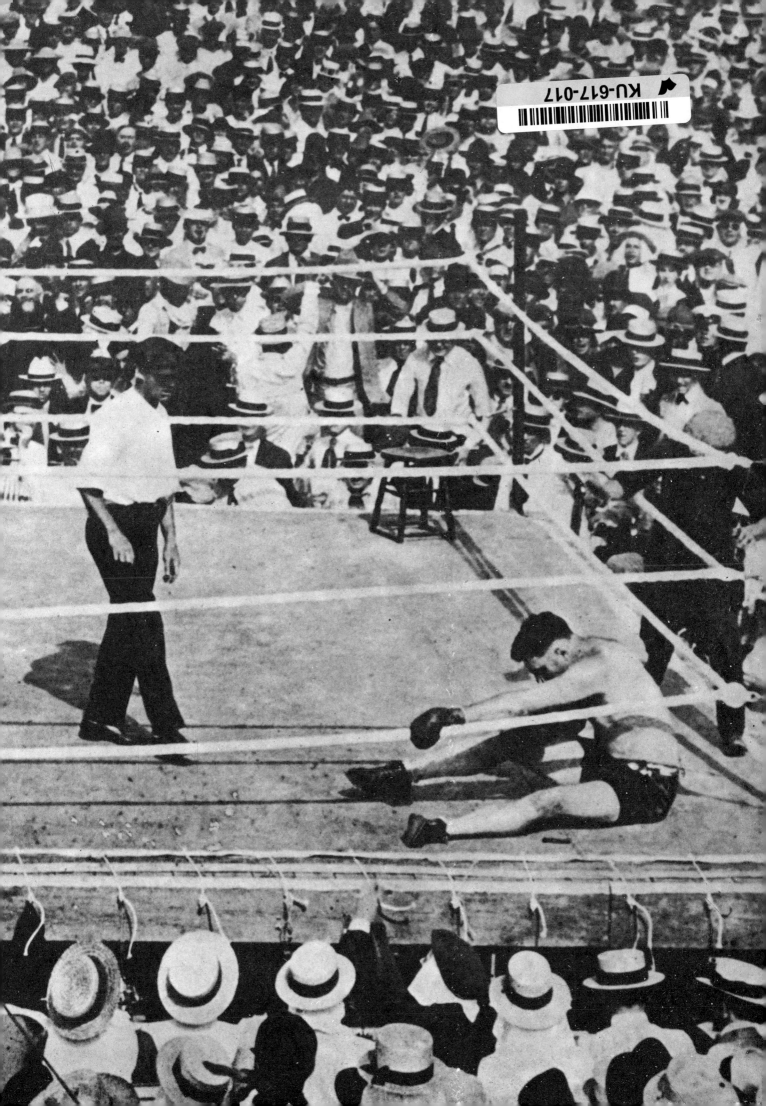

The Great
Heavyweights

The Great Heavyweights

Henry Cooper

Hamlyn
London New York Sydney Toronto

endpapers Jack Dempsey knocks down Jess Willard in the first round
of their championship fight.

half-title page Ingemar Johansson (left) is protected from Floyd Patterson
in their third match.

title page Muhammad Ali (right) attacks Floyd Patterson during their
first bout.

Published by
The Hamlyn Publishing Group Limited
London · New York · Sydney · Toronto
Astronaut House, Feltham, Middlesex, England

ISBN 0 600 34541 6

Printed in the U.K. by
R. J. Acford, Chichester
· Filmset in the U.K. by
Tradespools Limited, Frome

Contents

The Five Greats

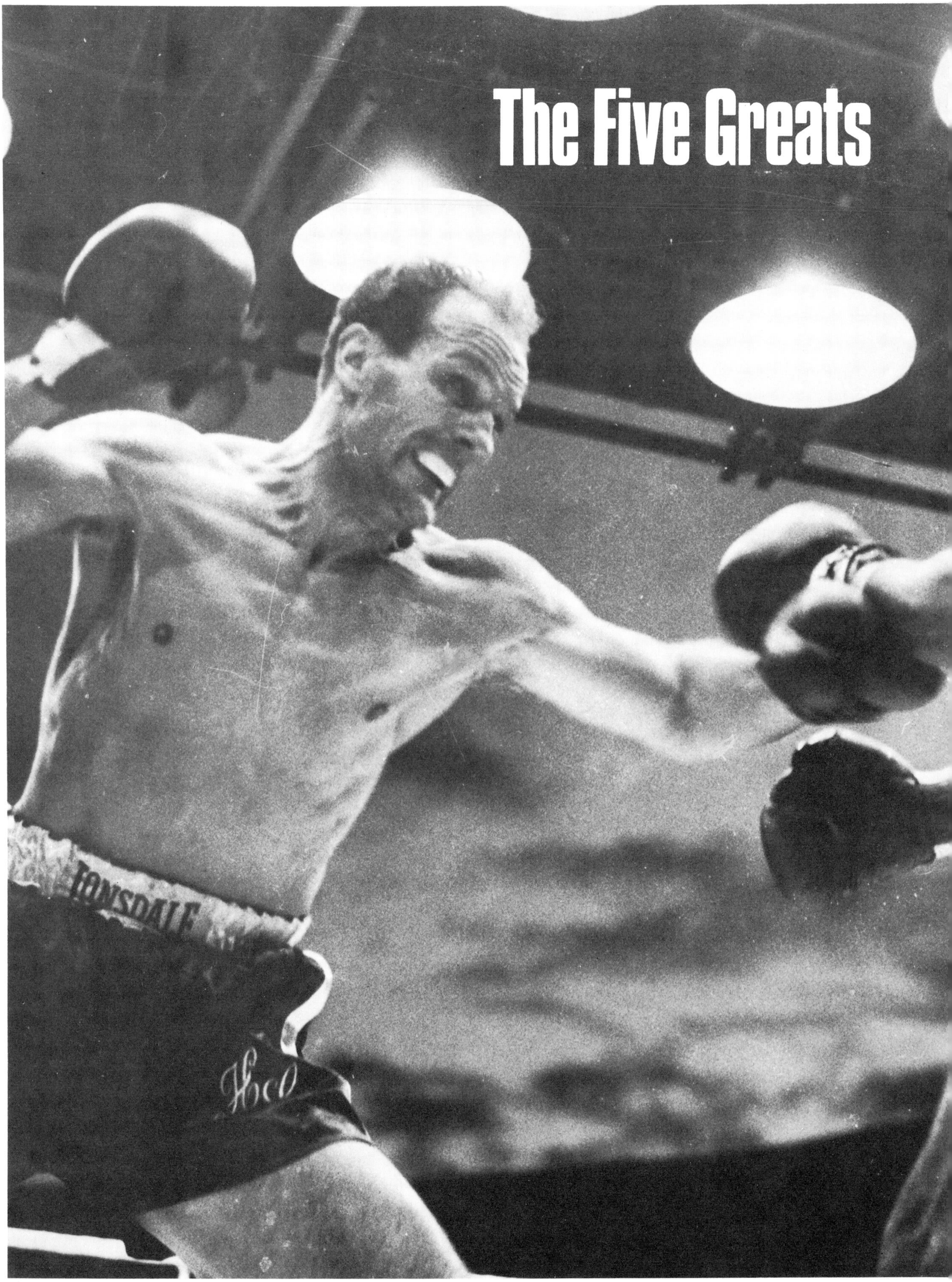

IN THE UNITED STATES, back in the old days when white was right and black was a decided disadvantage, they had a simple way of teaching the black boys how to fight. They'd toss half a dozen of them into the same ring and they'd fight each other until there was only one left standing on his feet.

Surrounded by the bodies of those who had been battered into oblivion, he'd be declared the champ. It was uncivilised. It was barbarous. But you've got to admit that using that system there's no way of arguing with the verdict.

It's all a bit different to the Eltham and District Boxing Club where my twin brother, George, and I learned our boxing, but I'm reminded about it every time somebody asks me who was the best heavyweight of all time. And I get asked that question more often than I used to get cut eyes when I was fighting.

In my opinion the five greatest heavyweights of all time were Jack Johnson, Jack Dempsey, Joe Louis, Rocky Marciano and Muhammad Ali, but I wouldn't like to decide which was the best. How would it be possible to separate these five without putting them into the same ring and letting them get on with it? And I wouldn't mind the television rights of that one!

Ali might start floating like a butterfly, but how many times would he be able to sting like a bee before one of the others caught up with him?

Rocky, his fists going like pistons, would be a one-man atom bomb until sheer exhaustion slowed him down.

Joe, calm and unruffled, would take everything they could throw at him without a change of expression, but would he get the chance to throw that blockbusting right?

Jack Dempsey, mean and merciless when there was one opponent in the ring, would need eyes in the back of that hard head.

And Jack Johnson, who learned his trade in those bloodbath rings of the Deep South where to survive was to win, would even his bull strength be enough?

I know this much. Outside the ring would be as near to it as I'd want to get!

They've got one thing going for them, these five, that can never be taken away from them. When they ruled the world the boxing game was at its best. And there's an old saying in boxing that the game is as good as the heavyweight champion.

When Jack Johnson was the king-pin, they turned up in their thousands to see the most hated man in the world hurt and humiliated. And he never was. Even when he lost his crown to Jess Willard, he admit-

Left **Henry Cooper attacking Muhammad Ali (then Cassius Clay) in their first fight on 18 June 1963.**

Right **Jack Johnson (World Champion 1908-1915).**

ted that he tossed it away for money. To understand the hatred that built up against Johnson, you have to understand the background. He was the first black man ever to become champion of the world. He'd grown up in Galveston on the Gulf of Mexico where the white man was king and the black man grovelled for what little he got. If the negro didn't want to spend the rest of his days lifting cotton bales, then he had to fight his way out.

Johnson did. And never forgot nor forgave the white man for the many insults he endured in his younger days.

The first sight of Johnson, fighting in a more upright style than we see now, that his opponent saw was a mouthful of gold teeth that couldn't be missed because his lips were always curled back in a sneer. My old manager, Jim Wicks, saw Johnson fight.

Right **Jack Johnson (right) evading a blow from middleweight champion Stanley Ketchel who was knocked out by Johnson in the 12th round.**

8

I'll take his word for it that the vision of Johnson, teeth glinting from a scowl as black as his face, was not exactly the sort of picture that Picasso would want to paint.

Many a time, Johnson could have knocked the guy out. But if his opponent was white he'd have to suffer. In those days, the 1890s and 1900s, referees didn't stop fights like they do now. A fighter would have to be half-dead before the referee would step in. And many of Johnson's opponents were!

But Johnson wasn't just a fighter. He was a boxer, too. And if anybody disputed it, Johnson had got a good punch to make his point. He couldn't have been as fast as Ali . . . who could? But although the Galveston Giant usually weighed-in at around 14st. (196 pounds) he could shift his feet a bit. The old-timers talked and talked well about his ability to slip punches and pick them out of the air.

On the way to becoming world champion, the mighty Johnson smashed Bob Fitzsimmons, the only British-born fighter ever to win the world heavyweight crown, into oblivion in two rounds. A year and a half after Johnson had won the title–and those were 18 months of misery to the white population of the United States–they dragged former champion James J. Jeffries into the ring again with the firm intention of putting the arrogant Johnson back in his black place.

Then they had to drag Jeffries out of the ring in the 15th round, a victim of thundering punches thrown between hurling insults at the whites at the ringside! They don't make them like that these days. Johnson and Ali would have been great together. But I can't help thinking that Muhammad has a nicer nature!

Jack Dempsey's start in life wasn't much better than Johnson's. He rode the railroad tracks as a hobo. The multi-dollar purses came later. It was cheaper to ride under the coaches than in them, and if you lost a leg under the wheels as one of his illicit travelling companions did, well . . .! Dempsey took risks in the ring, too. He was a fighter, not a boxer. Nobody gets to be heavyweight champion of the world without having a certain amount of skill. But Jack didn't seem to have an awful lot of confidence in it. He let his fists hammer out their own message, and if he had to trade punches, take two to land one, well the one that landed was going to be a good one.

Meet him in later years, as I did, a respected and successful businessman in his sixties and seventies, and it was almost impossible to imagine that in the ring he was all animal ferocity. How could it be with that gentle handshake, warm smile and appealing modesty?

But those old films tell a different tale. In Jack's fighting days they didn't, as they do now, send a boxer to a neutral corner while the count was going on. If the boxer had been taught the game properly, or learned the lesson from Jack, he stood behind the referee. Then, as the poor sucker reeled off the canvas wondering whether it was Christmas Day or Thanksgiving Day, he hung his sagging jaw straight into the flight path of high velocity leather.

By comparison, it's a gentleman's game these days, but I never heard any suggestion that Jack Dempsey ever apologised for his killer instinct.

The unique skill that Joe Louis had going

Below **Jack Dempsey (World Champion 1919-1926).**

9

Above **Jack Dempsey standing over a floored Luis Firpo. Firpo was put down a record nine times in the two-round fight.**

for him was that of sheer economy. It's not easy to put the point over to anyone who hasn't been deeply involved in boxing, but the amount of energy you use in a good fight would keep a couple of commandos in sweat for a week. So . . . you don't waste it. And Joe wasted less than any other world champion.

Muhammad Ali has the most extravagant and expensive of fighting styles. He burns up calories like they were going out of fashion. But Joe . . .! They didn't call him Shufflin' Joe for nothing. If he didn't have to shuffle three inches, then he wouldn't shuffle three inches. If four inches would get him out of trouble, then he never shuffled four and a half.

He was a beautiful mover, compact, and with a great left jab which more often than not opened the door for a right cross that might just as well have had the word curtains tattooed on the glove. If that wasn't enough, he could knock you dead with a left hook as well. It was all about

economy with Joe. There is no easier way of bringing an opponent's interest in a fight to an abrupt end than by setting him up with a left jab and then following it with a right cross.

There are still many people, all these years after, who say that Joe was the greatest of them all, and won't have it any other way. That's a matter of opinion. What is a matter of fact is that he held the world title longer than any other heavyweight . . . from June 1937 to March 1949. And as boxing teaches those of us who go in there and do the business to count, at least up to ten, I make that 12 years.

Twelve years at the top of the heap, the very top, is really mind-boggling even making allowances for the fact that war service in the United States army stopped him fighting in 1943-44-45. With a short break, I held the British heavyweight title for more than 12 years which puts me in a fair position to appreciate the magnitude of Joe's feat.

According to boxing's bible, 'The Ring' record book, Joe defended his title a record-breaking 25 times. In the late 1930s and early 1940s he was defending so often that they called it his 'Bum of the Month' campaign. Bums? If some of them had been fighting in later years they would have been world champions.

Joe always let his fists do his talking. He must have been an interviewer's nightmare. But a very genuine character.

In my time, there have only been two heavyweights Mums used to bring their babies to and ask the champion to hold them. One was Joe. The other was Rocky Marciano.

Rocky, the Brockton Blockbuster so tragically killed in an air crash the day before his 46th birthday, was a real Jekyll and Hyde character. There was never anybody quite like him in boxing. When he went into a ring he used to turn off. Or, as his hapless opponents would have to have it, turn on.

In the ring, Rocky never knew what he was doing. At least his day-to-day brain didn't. As soon as the gloves were taped on, the boxing brain took over. And as soon as the gloves were taken off, so his boxing brain switched off.

He was the only undefeated world champion. He had 49 fights, that's all, between 1947 and retirement in 1956. He won them all, 43 of them, yes 43, by knock-outs. And I doubt whether he could remember much about any of them. Outside the ring he was the most quiet, unassuming, inoffensive kind of guy you would wish to meet. I've seen him in a room, standing in a corner on his own. And he wouldn't say a word unless you spoke to him. But get him in a ring, and it was total warfare.

His character changed completely. He was so dedicated, so completely single-minded, that he didn't know what he was doing. Yet he came from quiet Italian stock, baptised with the very gentle-sounding name of Rocco Francis Marchegiano.

I remember when he fought Don Cockell in 1955. Don, from Battersea, an area of London slightly tougher than Bellingham where I was brought up, was British champion then, of course. He did his best fighting as a lightheavy before an attack of glandular fever forced his weight to go up. But, at that time, Don was full value for his chance for a crack at the world crown in Los Angeles.

Crack? There was certainly a crack as Rocky went in with his nut. Cockell came out of that one bleeding from the crown of

his head. Then, after Rocky's punches had brought Cockell to his knees, two more went into Don's face so late that they were nearly in time for Rocky's next fight. Eventually, the slaughter was stopped in the ninth. Don's defences had gone, and courage on its own just wasn't enough.

The Press boys poured down to Rocky's dressing-room. It was congratulations all the way round. Then somebody, with U.K. on his passport, asked Rocky why he hit Cockell when Don was on the deck.

Said Rocky: 'I didn't hit him when he was on the deck'. And he repeated it. Again and again. He just couldn't believe what he'd done. The reporters had to take him into a studio and rerun a film of the fight before Rocky stopped arguing.

Marciano had a fighting style all his own. He never risked a fight outside the United States. Teddy Waltham, who was then secretary of the British Boxing Board of Control and a referee good enough to take on world title fights, told Rocky flatly that

Above **Joe Louis in action against light-heavyweight Bob Pastor on 29 January 1937. Louis won on points over ten rounds.**

his way of fighting wouldn't be allowed in Britain.

I think he was a throwback to the old bareknuckle days. He must have been one of the hardest, most physically durable heavyweights of all time. And on top of that, if he missed you with a punch, then he'd be following through to get you with his elbow.

For a heavyweight, he was only a small man. He usually went into the ring at a

little over 13st. (182 pounds). But it was an awesome 13st.

I've always reckoned that physique was a legacy from his younger, pre-boxing days. He did a lot of labouring, digging ditches and all that sort of work. He built-up a lot of muscle around his shoulders, so much so that it was as though his head came out of his body. He didn't seem to have any neck. So when those fighters like Louis, Jersey Joe Walcott and one or two more – only one or two–gave him a bang on the whiskers, all that muscle just absorbed the shock.

I developed my biggest asset from similar circumstances, really. My Sunday punch, and I can say this without any false modesty, was the left hook . . . the one my mates in the Press seats nicknamed 'Enery's 'Ammer. I was rather fond of it. When I got it working properly, nine inches was all it needed to travel. Some useful jaws have felt it. Including Ali's.

But where did I develop it? Well, in my younger days, before brother George, who fought as Jim because there was another George Cooper around the rings at that time, and I took up boxing for a living we were plasterers, among several other jobs.

But plasterer was what I used to call myself on my income tax returns . . . when we earned enough to qualify for tax. Reg Reynolds, who became a relation when his daughter Barbara married George, was the bloke who taught us plastering, how to mix the stuff, how to throw it against the wall, how to level it, and all the rest. In those days remember, what we were using was cement, sand and lime. Take my word for it, it gets heavy and it wants some pushing around. So I pushed it, and pushed it–all day long.

I'm left-handed, and I'll bet you've got the message straight away. All that pushing really developed the left side of my body, the trunk and the shoulders. So it didn't do me any harm to carry on plastering for the first eighteen months of my professional career until it became impossible for me to carry on with the two occupations.

Later on, different trainers and masseurs, whenever I had a rub-down, remarked on the left side of my body. It was far more muscular than the right. Same with tennis players. Their racquet arms can look twice as big as the other arm. Rod Laver's did, I believe.

Mind you, I don't use my left hand much these days though it does come in handy for endorsing cheques. It's that 'Ammer that's the cause of it. When I was around 26, I had to have the left hand X-rayed.

The doctors had a look, and then another good look. Then they told me that it showed the wear of a man of 70! You can't blame me for being careful with it, can you?

Muhammad Ali will never have the same trouble. He doesn't punch hard enough. I should know. I fought him twice–when he was at his peak.

What Ali was, at his best, was the fastest moving heavyweight of all time. There have been heavier punchers, just one or two quicker punchers. But nobody has in the

past, or ever will in the future, moved around the ring as fast as Ali. In that respect he was well entitled to call his life story 'The Greatest'.

We're talking about a big man, here. He's 6ft. 3in. and his weight has been about 16st. (224 pounds). In natural attributes he's a super heavyweight and usually when a man's that build his movements are slower and so are his reflexes.

There's a myth about weight. People used

Above **Rocky Marciano (World Champion 1952-1956).**

13

to say to me that if I'd have been a stone heavier I'd have done this and have been able to do that. I don't agree. When I was within a pound of 13½st. (189 pounds), which was my best fighting weight, I was moving faster than at any time in my career. I used to love going in with a guy who was a stone and a half heavier. By the time they'd had a big wind up to hit me the chances are that I'd been in, landed a punch, and nipped back out of distance.

Now, if I could do that, imagine taking on Ali who was such an exception to the big man rule. He was in and out like a welterweight, and he had this unique thing going for him: he was born with it.

It was his natural ability and style. I could have spent 24 hours a day training and trying to copy it and got nowhere because it wasn't natural to me. But it was to Ali. It was just one of those phenomenal things.

But punching power? No. I've looked at fights and marvelled when he's knocked those big guys down and they've rolled over on their backs.

In those two fights, both in London, in 1963 and again in 1966 when it was for the world championship, I went the best, or the worst whichever way you look at it, part of 11 rounds with Ali. And the only time he ever got aggressive, the only time he really came forward slinging punches was in the first one when I had my eye so badly slit.

I had blood pouring in the eye. It was coming in so fast I couldn't see. He knew it. So he came forward. Punch after punch. He hit me on the chin . . . two or three times. But I didn't go down. I wasn't really hurt. He certainly wanted to finish it there and then. And he did. But it was the blood and not the count. I've been hit harder, much harder, by a dozen heavyweights who were better punchers.

Normally, I'm an Ali man. I think he's been great for boxing. He's kept the game alive when it could have been dying. All those boasts, or outrageous statements as I prefer to regard them, were made for the box-office. Boxing's never had anybody like him for selling his own fights.

But he wasn't on the level, and I repeat

Below **A right uppercut from Rocky Marciano to the head of Ezzard Charles in Marciano's points win over the former champion.**

that I admire the guy, when he made out after that first fight that he didn't like hitting Cooper when he'd seen that blood.

I ought to know. I was taking the punches. And there's plenty of film evidence to back me when I say that he kept back out of the way until he could see the blood pumping into my eye. Then he got confident. Then he started coming into me because he knew that, though he was within range, the blurred vision was affecting my judgement of my punches.

It was one round earlier when I'd made my own bit of boxing history by becoming one of the few men, at that time certainly, to put Ali on the canvas. And if I'd managed it a few seconds earlier then he wouldn't have got up a second time.

The eye, the left one, had been badly cut in the third round. My corner was talking about stopping the fight, but I talked them out of it. I had a feeling I could nail him if I could get inside.

Now that wasn't easy because the second of Ali's great assets, and one which no other boxer can surely have possessed to the same degree, was the ability to judge distances. With those marvellous reflexes, he knew to an inch when he was safely out of range.

He could swivel from the hips. That in itself is unorthodox, but Ali had done everything unorthodoxly since he was a kid. When you're taught boxing, you don't sway out of the way and lean back out of punches. You come forward inside a punch. You slip punches. Ali did practically everything wrong but he could get away with it because of those reflexes, that swivel and the speed of his footwork.

He could drop his hands and do all that clamour because he knew he was just out of distance. As I say, even to an inch.

And that's what he was doing in that dramatic fourth round, dancing away, just out of reach. Or so he thought. I showed him one left and he went back towards the ropes. I showed him two lefts and back he went again, nearer the ropes. I showed him three lefts and he was back as far as he could go.

I knew I had the ability. My good punch was being able to hook off the jab. So I went bump, bump, bump, and then got him with the hook because he couldn't go back any further. That's how he got caught. Going back, doing it his way. But if he'd been boxing like everybody else boxes instead of trying to keep his jaw just an inch out of the range of my fists, he would have been coming forward instead of going backwards and he wouldn't have been caught by my punch.

But once the punch had landed, Ali's

being on the ropes was the factor that went against me. Half the time when you hit guys like I'd just hit Ali, it's the actual shock of when they hit the deck that does the damage. And if their head hits the canvas as well, it has practically the same effect as a punch . . . it scrambles their brains a bit and they don't know where they are.

When I hit Ali he had a soft fall. He went from the top rope to the middle and then to the bottom. His fall was broken. If only I'd caught him in the middle of the ring . . . he'd have gone down in a heap, and he might not have been able to get up.

Ali has a touch of the Jack Johnsons in his make-up. With certain opponents who'd upset him, or for some reason he had no time for, he'd an arrogant, some would say even a cruel streak.

The classic example was Floyd Patterson. Even though Floyd had been world champion, Ali had no time for him. The first time they met, Ali toyed with Floyd for 12 rounds, and they were 12 rounds of sheer torture. That was for Ali's world title in 1965. Seven years later they met again, no titles this time. Ali was kinder. He put Floyd away in seven rounds.

Maybe they would have appreciated Ali's hard streak back in the cock-pit rings of the Deep South. I would think so. You don't become one of the five all-time greats if you include the word mercy in your boxing dictionary.

Jack Johnson

EAST-SIDE

DANA
Photo.S.F.

KETCHEL. — JOHNSON.

Leaned By
Bertillon

Many words have been used about Jack Johnson. Poor, rich, idolised, hated. Yes, all those. But probably arrogant is the one that sums him up best. Born John Arthur Johnson, he liked to call himself 'L'il Arthur', and the fact that he became the first negro to become world heavyweight champion should have been enough to ensure his immortality.

But Johnson had chips from the time he discovered there were shoulders to wear them on. And his shoulders were never bare.

He must have been a strange contradiction. He was born in the slum areas of Galveston. He had no social advantages. Yet he taught himself to speak French, German and Spanish fluently.

His insistence that his main object in life was to put the white man in his place became an obsession. He was rude and crude. He had a temper that seemed permanently on a short fuse. Yet he also had a sense of humour, in the right place.

Once, in London, Johnson was accosted by a drunk who shouted: 'You niggers are all yellow-livered. You don't like being hit in the belly'. Johnson had put men in hospital for less than that. Those within earshot winced and waited.

But Johnson just said: 'You're right. But do you know any white fellas who like being hit in the same place twice?' But above all else, Johnson had one absolute asset. He was very brainy, shrewdly not necessarily academically. You had to be, I suppose, to get out of the negro ghettos.

Jim Wicks, my old manager, saw Johnson fight, way, way back. He tells me that Johnson and Ali have a lot in common. For a start, both were very full of themselves. And Jim says Johnson could do what Ali could do, and that is be so in command of a fight that he could virtually finish it when he liked.

I get the impression from Jim that Johnson was probably a better boxer than most people give him credit for. He wasn't as fast as Ali – now that is asking something – but he could make people miss, and he was a master at picking punches out of the air.

Like Ali he could laugh at an opponent. Like Ali again, he could take time off from a fight to shout, usually taunts in Johnson's case, to the audience. And there was one thing he could do better than Ali, even. And that's punch. There was a knock-out in both of the Johnson fists.

With all that going for him, Johnson should have been a hero. But he was despised. Not surprising, really. His first wife was a negro. The others, and there were

Left **Stanley Ketchel puts Jack Johnson down in the 12th round of their bout in Colma, California. The enraged champion immediately got up to knock Ketchel out with an uppercut which broke several of Ketchel's teeth.**

Above **Jack Johnson complete with gold teeth.**

But I'm sure who the boss man must have been.

The Galveston Giant first threw his fists in anger, for money anyway, in 1897. By 1902 he'd punched his way out of Texas, and was undefeated in 47 bouts until he tangled with Marvin Hart who was to become the least-known world heavyweight champion of them all later in 1905.

Hart and Johnson went 20 rounds. Hart nicked the points and Johnson wasn't pleased. Hart soon lost the title to French-Canadian Tommy Burns and Johnson demanded to know when it was going to be his turn for a crack at the world crown.

Burns was less than keen. Johnson was piling up another unbroken sequence spoiled only when a referee with astonishing courage disqualified Johnson for fouling a certain Joe Jeannette in the second round. Later, Jeannette paid for it in pain.

Burns didn't need the situation spelling out. He decided that the rest of the world deserved a chance to see the champion and London looked a sight more appetising than a roaring Johnson.

While Burns was beating England's Gunner Moir and Jack Palmer, Johnson added up his cash and followed Burns to England. Too late. Burns had remembered two things. One that he was the smallest man, at only 5ft. 7in., to hold the world title and the other was that every time Johnson had hammered a white boxer, there'd been race riots. People had died.

In the circumstances there was only one decision, and Burns made it. It was Australia, with a stop off on the way in Paris. It was the story of Johnson's life at that time. Always one stop behind Burns.

Johnson had his couple of fights in Plymouth. They kept the wolf from the door, but Australia was a long way away, and it was going to cost to get there. There was an attempt to match him with British champion-to-be Bombardier Billy Wells, but the Home Office refused permission for the fight to go on.

That's how it was that Johnson went on the halls, to make money to pay for his journey to Australia. He also thought of another way. Peggy Bettinson, the 'guv'nor' of the National Sporting Club, which virtually ran boxing in Britain before the Boxing Board of Control was formed in 1929, listened to the Johnson line in chat and agreed to lend him the fare to the other side of the world on the understanding that when he had won the title—there were no ifs about Johnson—he'd come back and defend it. He never did.

several, all had this in common—they were white girls. And at the turn of the century and on into the twenties, inter-racial marriage didn't get you to the post in the social stakes.

But that didn't bother Johnson one little bit. Between boxing, he ran night clubs in Chicago, packed music-halls in Europe, and even did a year in jail for skipping over the state line with an under-age white girl. The years he spent in Britain immediately before losing his title to Jess Willard in 1915 were different—for Britain. One of the sights of London, according to Jim Wicks, was a golden trilby and crocodile shoes adorning either end of Johnson.

But that all came later, when he was in the middle of running through eight managers. What it must have been like to have managed such a character I can't imagine.

But Johnson was on his way, and the anti-white feeling was stoked by an incident at the National Sporting Club where he had been asked to spar to show members what he could do. The request angered Johnson who thought it deliberately insulting. In view of this, then perhaps Bettinson should not have been surprised at the treatment he got from Johnson.

Johnson was so keen to get Burns within striking distance of his fists that he would have paid money almost for the chance to get in the same ring. And he did. He accepted 1,500 dollars for the fight. Burns got 32,000 dollars.

But there was still one bridge to cross. Johnson was taking no chances with the referee. He knew the score and reckoned there was no way they were going to let a black man outpoint a white man. Also,

Above **Tommy Burns' last title defence in the United States before his world tour to avoid Johnson. Burns (right) knocked out Bill Squires in the first round. The referee in the centre is former champion James J. Jeffries.**

Left **Jim Flynn, a fireman who unsuccessfully fought Tommy Burns and Jack Johnson for the world title. He later knocked out Jack Dempsey in one round.**

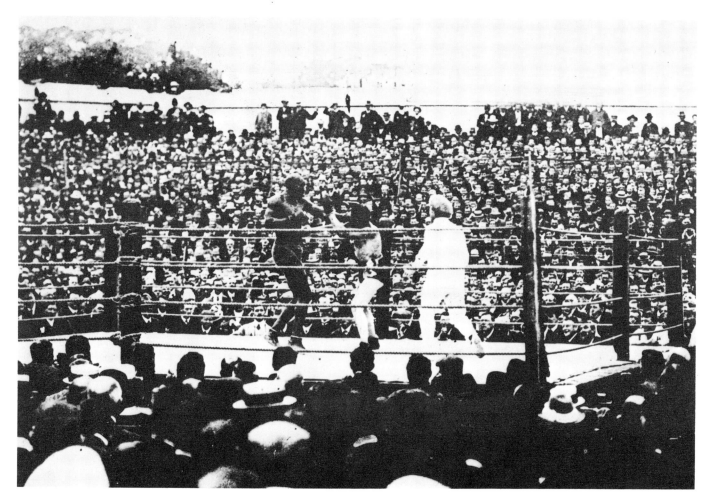

Above The fight at Rushcutters Bay, Sydney in which Jack Johnson (left) beat Tommy Burns to become world heavyweight champion. Johnson was 20 pounds heavier than Burns and almost six inches taller.

Right Burns (foreground) facing Johnson. Johnson gave Burns a terrible beating.

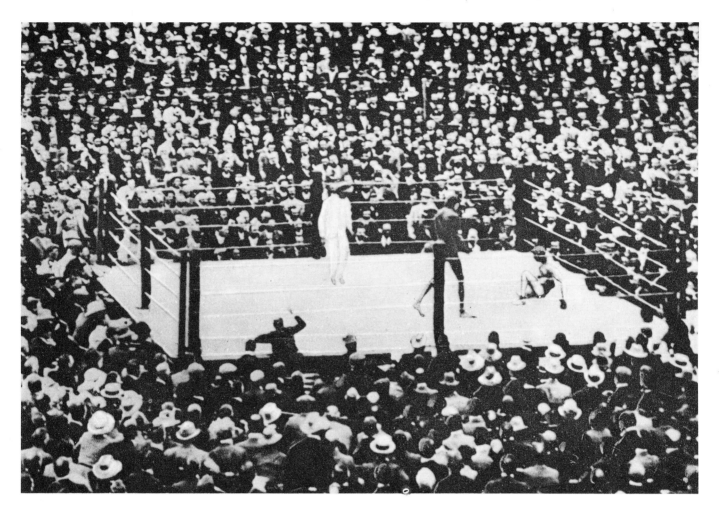

Burns was the favourite. So, after rejecting man after man, Johnson finally agreed to the promoter, Hugh McIntosh, refereeing the fight. It was one way McIntosh could be sure that Johnson would step inside the ropes at Rushcutters Bay, Sydney, on the Boxing Day of 1908.

But, before they started, there's the lovely story about the gentleman out of Sydney's social top drawer who had been an amateur boxer of some standing. So he knew the game, he supposed. And laid on a super party to celebrate Burns' victory. It was a dinner party for a couple of dozen and enough champagne to take care of everybody's thirst. After Johnson's victory, our fella left the ringside like he was the one who had been taking all the punishment, and walked home in a trance. When he got there, he went straight to bed leaving his guests to get on with it. His hospitality was in no danger. Every member of his party was similarly afflicted! Nobody came to the party.

Not that Burns knew anything about it after what is generally agreed to have been one of the most brutal fights in history. Officially, the records just say: won in the 14th. It seems as if Burns, courageous to the end, avoided the knock-out. He didn't.

Johnson did. 'L'il Arthur' could have finished it almost any time he liked. But he wouldn't. It was the police who eventually stepped in, to save the stricken champion suffering.

At 30 years of age, Johnson had cracked it. After nine years in the ring, 'L'il Arthur' was the heavyweight champion of the world. What could he do to follow that? Easy. He had one of his gold teeth stopped with a diamond!

That gesture didn't win him any medals back home in the States. They were frantically looking for a White Hope. But they were having to face the fact that the first black man to take the world crown had exceptional speed, was an outstanding tactician, could punch hard enough to damage an opponent's forearm, and could stop a man dead with the power of a punch to the bicep. And if that wasn't enough to be getting on with, Johnson had mastered the technique of a punch that looked as though it was going into the belly when it started but finished up thudding against the throat.

There were minor skirmishes inside the ring that never added up to Johnson being in danger of losing his title. Once, middle-weight Stan Ketchel made the mistake of

Above **Burns on the canvas near the end of the fight, which the police stopped in the 14th round to prevent further punishment.**

Right Johnson being introduced to the crowd before his match with James J. Jeffries on 4 July 1910.

Below The return to the ring of former champion James J. Jeffries, then 35, in an attempt to defeat Jack Johnson. Johnson won in 15 rounds.

flooring Johnson. The angry champion climbed off the canvas and let go a left that put Ketchel straight into never-never land.

There were major skirmishes outside the ring where Johnson's outrageous mode of life was turning him into the most hated man in the United States.

Then, they thought they'd found the way to sort Johnson out. In 1910 they induced James J. Jeffries, the former world No. 1, to come out of retirement and do everybody a favour. It was a colossal mistake. Jeffries hadn't fought for six years. It really was lamb to the slaughter. And Johnson enjoyed every minute. He'd been enjoying it for weeks, if the truth were known, because he had been deliberately allowing the rumour to spread that he thought it so easy that he hadn't bothered to do any proper training.

Not for the first time, and certainly not for the last, was Johnson conning the great American public. Hugh McIntosh, the man who had promoted the Burns fight, was in Reno for the Jeffries fight and was betting

with thousands of dollars of Johnson money, snatching at the odds as they lengthened slightly as the news of Johnson's apparent lack of total fitness was allowed to get around.

What was really happening was that Johnson, having let himself be seen to be out of condition, then retired gracefully from the public eye and did his training at night. There was nothing wrong with him when he got into the ring.

It was Independence Day, 1910, and it must have been one of the greatest days of Johnson's life. He looked down at the whites who'd come just to see him beaten, but he knew there was no way he could lose and from his corner he flung his jibes at them. Despite the intensity of the hate campaign Johnson knew he could get away with it. Because they'd all been made to leave their guns outside the arena.

The authorities just had to make that rule. Otherwise some liquored-up character would have been more than capable of sending a bullet in Johnson's direction.

Six years of idleness had done nothing for Jeffries' legs, nor for his stomach muscles. At 35, he was too long gone from the action. Johnson was in one of his meanest moods and Jeffries suffered almost as much as Burns had done in Sydney. Johnson was going to twist the knife, and twist it he did. There must have been opportunities to knock out the old champion, but Johnson wasn't having any.

The name of the game was humiliation. Jeffries' handlers and backers had even gone to the trouble to get the legendary James J. Corbett, who had been world champion for five years before losing the title to Bob Fitzsimmons in 1897, to act as advisor. And Johnson, pausing from time to time in the destruction of Jeffries, had himself a ball hurling insults at one of boxing's greatest names.

Not that Jeffries knew much about it, or could do much about it. Remarkably, Jeffries kept coming out for each round, but in the 15th the towel came fluttering in. Jeffries couldn't take any more.

Left **Frank Moran (left) dominated the first half of his fight with Johnson, but was outpointed over 20 rounds. The referee was Georges Carpentier, the future world light-heavyweight champion.**

23

Life inside the ring might have been easy for Johnson. But outside, it was getting more and more harrassing.

There was the aftermath of his victory over Jeffries. It stirred up the hatred between black and white right across the American continent. In New York's Harlem, no white man ventured if he had any sense. Negro homes were razed and burned in several states. Clashes on street corners were legion. And, dreadfully, in some towns and outposts torchlight processions hunted and hanged negroes simply because a black man had beaten a white man.

There was more than enough trouble there for one man to live with. And over Johnson's head was still the charge of abduction. So after fighting and beating Jim Flynn in Las Vegas he eventually made his way to Europe. In his absence he was

tried, found guilty and sentenced to a year's imprisonment.

He had several fights while he was in Europe, including one against Frank Moran, a Pittsburgh dentist, in Paris.

And the story of that fight, as it has been handed down to me, tells it all about what kind of character Johnson was.

That fight was different in several respects. First of all it was refereed by Georges Carpentier, then well on his way to becoming the darling of France. The Johnson fight was on 27 June 1914. And Carpentier gave Johnson the verdict on points over 20 rounds.

Right, 19 days later Georges fought Gunboat Smith in London, grabbed the verdict when Smith was disqualified for a foul in the sixth round—and then claimed the white heavyweight title of the world!

Right **Jack Johnson.**

That was one aspect of the Johnson-Moran fight. Another was that this seems to have been the first time the ladies attended a fight in force. Boxing was on the way to becoming a social occasion.

It's as well to know, too, that Moran possessed a hell of a right uppercut, that he called Mary Anne, and it had seen off 14 opponents before their time. Then there was Johnson, getting on a bit. He was 36, the same age as Jeffries had been when Johnson had sorted him out. This time, Johnson really was out of condition so nobody, least of all Johnson, was seeing this as an easy one for the champ.

Johnson himself recognised the danger. The deal he proposed was simple enough. Moran would get 40 per cent of half of the gate as his purse . . . if he laid down in the eighth. If he didn't, then Moran wouldn't get anything.

Moran got the message, and pondered. He didn't like it. So he sorted out promoter Theodore Vienne to get his reaction. It was

predictable. Vienne had spent huge sums on the fight. If it didn't go on, he was set to lose a fortune. So Moran sent the message back that he was agreeing to Johnson's terms.

It was a shock for Johnson then that as they touched gloves Moran told him that the contest was on the level.

I'm told there was fear on the face of Johnson. Certainly he had to be in big trouble. He was outboxed in the early rounds and then in the fifth, his big chance arrived. Carpentier ordered a clean break. Johnson took no notice. He had hold of Moran's head and smashed his nose with a crunching uppercut. Moran the dentist was getting first hand the feeling of what it is like to be swallowing your own blood.

It was an obvious foul, but Carpentier took no action other than warning Johnson that he would be disqualified if he did it again. He didn't have to. Moran was slowed right down. He lasted the 20 rounds, and as Johnson, not surprisingly, had improved during the second half of the bout, he got Carpentier's verdict.

Now we get to the fun bit. Moran was up early in the morning to collect his share of the spoils from the promoter. But Johnson's creditors – he was absolutely broke – had been up earlier and had been in first. Under French law they were entitled to collect. And they had.

So poor Moran even had to pay to get his nose fixed. If Moran had beaten Johnson, there was no possible way either Carpentier or Smith would have been able to call himself the white heavyweight champion of the world. Because the real heavyweight champ would have been Moran who was white.

Johnson moved on. He fought in Buenos Aires. He came back to Europe. Anywhere except the United States which he'd left in 1912. There was still that year's imprisonment hanging over his head.

Back in the States the situation was grim. Nobody was making any money out of the world title. It was the same in Europe where the ageing Johnson wasn't making much out of it either.

So, early in 1915 there was a meeting between promoter Jack Curley, representing a bunch of wealthy New Yorkers, and Johnson. Would Jack come home and defend the title against Jess Willard, the latest of the white hopes? But they'd been through that movie before. United States meant arrest.

Then they fed Johnson the story that he might have the sentence waived if he came back and lost to Willard. Johnson wasn't swallowing that one, and stipulated that the fight would be in Mexico over 20 rounds. Next, Johnson heard that he might be the victim of a kidnapping plot and had the contest switched to Cuba where it had to be over 45 rounds.

The suggestion that Johnson might be granted a pardon is not as outrageous as it might seem. As black champion, in the climate of those days, he had no chance of any favours. But if he was a party to the world title going back to a white man . . . that made some sort of sense. To Johnson, at least.

Then, according to Johnson, his fee for the fight was to be paid to his wife sitting by the ringside. And there was also a deal giving him certain film rights.

The actual truth, as in most circumstances, probably lies somewhere between the two extremes. But, if Johnson did have to lose the fight, why would he wait until the 26th round, for that was when Willard knocked him out? Then, surely, nobody was going to pass a parcel of money amounting to anything between 25,000 and 35,000 dollars to a woman sitting at the ringside. She could hardly stuff that in her handbag and stroll out with it.

Johnson always alleged that he dived. But he was out in front until the 20th round. Willard had suffered a deep cut on his right cheek as early as the ninth, and to me that would seem to indicate that Johnson wasn't exactly just trying to lose it.

At the end of the day, the likelihood is that advancing fighting years and lack of condition caught up with Johnson.

And what is significant is that, after losing the fight, Johnson didn't go back to the States. His fight film had been banned there, and he went back to Europe to try and sell it. From what I can make out, Johnson was much more successful as a fighter than a seller of film.

He stayed in Europe, fighting in Spain and occasionally, because money is money, even fighting the bulls. By 1920, Johnson had crossed the Atlantic again. This time the destination was Mexico City. Johnson was into his 42nd year now, but still good enough to get into a ring and give value for money.

Yet he'd been a long time away from the States. Eight years. So in the middle of 1920, Johnson crossed the border and gave himself up. Any ideas that the law would tell him to forget it were quickly killed off. He was sent to a penitentiary in Kansas.

Johnson's hideaway? Not on your life. Not only did he soon become the gaol's No. 1 personality, they actually brought boxers in for him to fight! Semi-exhibitions they might have been, but . . . that was Johnson!

On and on he went. In May 1928 he fought his last proper, serious, down-in-the-record-books fight. He was knocked out in six rounds. Not too bad, all things considered. It was 13 years since he'd lost the world title. And he was a couple of months beyond his 50th birthday. If I'm putting gloves on at that age, they'll only be golf gloves, I promise you.

But years later Johnson was wearing gloves again. He boxed six one-minute exhibition rounds in New York. He was 67. A few weeks after his 68th birthday, the world mourned the old champion. He always drove his cars fast. He swerved off the road and crashed. A few hours after being pulled from the wrecked car he died in a North Carolina hospital, a legend long before his own lifetime had run its course.

Above **In 1936 Johnson, then 59, appeared as an Ethiopian general in a performance of 'Aida' by the New York Hippodrome Opera Company. The role didn't include singing, but Johnson did display his fighting ability on stage.**

27

Jack Dempsey

JACK DEMPSEY, world heavyweight champion from July, 1919 when he massacred Jess Willard until outpointed by Gene Tunney in September, 1926, was a fighter the boxing public never shed tears for – in his fighting days. For Jack, now utterly revered in the United States, was hated when he was in the ring.

There was a misguided belief that he'd settled for boxing, during the days of the First World War, instead of going into the services. But the anti-Dempseys had got it wrong. Jack was married at the time, and because of that it was ruled that he was exempt from call-up on the grounds that he was supporting a wife.

Dempsey, and he admits it quite honestly these days, is one of those characters just born to fight. His is something of a rags to riches story though really it was only Jack that was broke, not his parents. He rode the railroads, surely that part of the Dempsey legend is true. But there is plenty of evidence from Jack himself that he did not grow up wondering where the next crust was coming from.

He just made up his mind when he was around thirteen years old that he was going to become a fighter, though the determination may have stemmed from his being turfed off a train with his mother, brother and sister because he looked, to put it generously, too big to pay a half fare, and the family hadn't got quite enough – it was a long journey – to afford full fare for Jack.

So he worked in the mines and lumber camps to strengthen his muscles, toughened his jaw by chewing gum, and hardened his fists by giving them the traditional pickle in brine treatment.

Jack needed that because as world heavyweight champions go he wasn't all that big. He had the height, 6ft. 1½in. between the top of his head and the soles of his feet. But even in his prime there was no more weight than 14st. (196 pounds) at the most. In fact he mostly fought at somewhere near 190 pounds.

That is why I always say that you don't have to be a big super heavyweight. I think that size, if you are very big, can be a great disadvantage. Dempsey, in his prime, was always a lean and hungry guy, but a killer once he got into the ring.

When you got down to the basics, with Jack it was all ferocity. And, like all the greats, he didn't like his opponents.

If you've seen films of those old fights, you may have noticed that they didn't send boxers to a neutral corner while a count was going on. They did before Dempsey's

Left **Dempsey stretching to deliver a right to Willard. Despite conceding over 50 pounds and five inches in height, Dempsey hammered the champion into submission in three rounds.**

career was to end, and his failure to go to a neutral corner had dramatic effects, but more about that later.

When Dempsey launched himself on an unsuspected boxing world the drill was simple. The boxer who had delivered the punch that put the other fellow down would stand behind the referee, waiting. And when the poor sucker got off the deck he'd get another faceful of glove before he was ready to defend himself.

If you don't like it, then blame the rules, not the Dempseys of this world. And it's still, even in this day and age, a hit or get hit game.

And Jack, surely one of the nicest fellas this game of ours has ever produced, never made an apology for anything that happened inside the ropes.

But to get back to what I mean about heavyweights and their build, have a good look at the pictures of Dempsey. You'll see very long arms, and very powerful shoulders. And the eyes, because of some Red Indian ancestry, are extremely deep set. As a boxer who suffered from cuts too often at vital moments in my career, I can envy the protection Dempsey's eyes had from his bones!

Then have a look at Jack's waist. It is slender enough not to disgrace a dancer. And the legs taper to the proportions of a track athlete. In later years he thickened. But don't we all? And that build allowed him to cut Willard to ribbons. Indeed, plenty of ringside fans wanted it stopped after the first round. The same thing happened to Georges Carpentier, the Frenchman who was a natural light-heavyweight and a world champion of that division. He was the Orchid Man who had his petals ripped off one by painful one by a Dempsey who showed absolutely no mercy. The fans took pity again when Dempsey fought Luis Firpo in 1923. Hardly surprising. Firpo, an Argentinean known as the Wild Bull of the Pampas, was tamed in Tom and Jerry cartoon fashion by hitting the deck nine times. And the fight didn't last two rounds. Sadistic was the word they threw about.

When the punches were going in, forearms working like pistons, Dempsey was the most exciting heavyweight since John

Below **Jess Willard under attack from challenger Jack Dempsey in the first round of their title fight on 4 July 1919. The challenger floored Willard seven times in this round, but was unable to keep him down.**

L. Sullivan drew on gloves. He was involved with Carpentier in the first million dollar gate, and he topped the million four more times. In the 1920s, that was real money. It would be worth five or six times as much these days.

Figures like that are a long, long way away from the Mormon background in which Jack grew up in Manassa, Colorado. He had eight elder brothers and sisters and two younger, so the money had to be looked at before it was spent. Ask Jack what he is and he'll insist that he's Irish. But I'm told that the Indian blood is really Cherokee, and he's not without a trace of Jewish, too.

I suppose with a background like that, Jack had to become champion of the world. There could hardly be a single part of it he could qualify to be champion of.

The Dempsey family trekked from one side of Colorado to the other, and young Jack earned what he could on the way. When he could, he left home. Wanderlust set in early. He worked on a farm, down a copper mine, had a stint as a lumberjack, and with sheer irony, sharpened his punching ability as a bouncer!

By the time he was in his middle teens Dempsey was fighting for cash. Or trying to. I gather in those days there was a tendency to pay the winners and tip the losers. Dempsey, calling himself Kid Blackie, didn't eat so well.

But he picked up a couple of stories he told repeatedly. He fought a character named Two Round Gilhan in Salt Lake City. This time the said Mr Gilhan lasted less than one round! And there was One Punch Hancock. Dead right. Only the punch was delivered by J. Dempsey, Esq . . .!

They didn't seem to want to know Dempsey in New York – then. (Later, many years later, New Yorkers were to pack into his famous Broadway restaurant for years.) So Jack took himself off to Philadelphia. He arrived there without even the price of a hot dog.

Back in Salt Lake City a character named Jim Flynn had the temerity to knock the future world champion down four times in the first round, and Jack wasn't to hear the bell for the second round. It wasn't necessary. Twelve months later the same Mr Flynn was belted into oblivion, also in

Below **Jess Willard on the canvas near the end of the first round of his fight with Jack Dempsey (left). Dempsey thought the champion had been counted out and left the ring, but in fact the bell had saved Willard and Dempsey had to be recalled by his manager, Doc Kearns, who is shown climbing into the ring.**

less than a round. Revenge might have been sweet, but before that the money wasn't coming in.

Jack had had a look at what he did best, and was working down the Californian iron mines and telling his manager Doc Kearns that he was quitting boxing. Then Kearns, who became a millionaire, made the momentous decision of his life. He told Jack to spend three months in Seattle, working in the navy yard, and to forget about boxing. It worked. Jack got his old adrenalin running again, and from then on it was all one way.

He fought 21 times in 1918 during which he ran up a string of five successive first round knock-outs. In fact 12 of those 21 opponents lost all interest inside three rounds. Dempsey had to fight so often to get the rust off his ringcraft.

July 27 has its little place in history. Fred Fulton, called the Sepulpa Plasterer, was plastered in 18 seconds. Then came December 16 and a quick introduction to Carl Morris. Morris could justifiably claim: 'What fight?'. Really, he missed it, because it only lasted 14 seconds and that included the count. He must have blinked for four seconds.

By now, Dempsey was the logical challenger to champion Jess Willard. But Jack had to wait for the fight. They were building

a special stadium in Toledo to take it.

Promoter Tex Rickard was then just about the biggest name in boxing. Christened George Lewis and brought up on a Texas ranch after being orphaned at ten years old, Tex had just about been everything. Cowboy, horse-breaker, sheriff. Then he went prospecting in the Klondyke gold rush, which is where he met manager Doc Kearns. He became the owner of a saloon and one of the great gamblers.

By the time the negotiations for Dempsey to fight Willard were concluded, Rickard needed something like 150,000 dollars to break even. And Rickard wanted profit, big profit.

So, at Toledo, Ohio in the midwest, Rickard found the timber and built his own stadium. There was seating for 80,000 with room for another 20,000 standing. The temperature was 100 degrees, and Rickard was the only one who wasn't sweating. Before the fight started, he knew he'd taken more than 400,000 dollars.

Willard was the tallest man ever to win the world championship. This was 1919 and Jess had been a hero with the United States white population for four years since acquiring the title from hated negro Jack Johnson. He was also fighting at something like 17½st. (245 pounds), more than 50 pounds more than Dempsey.

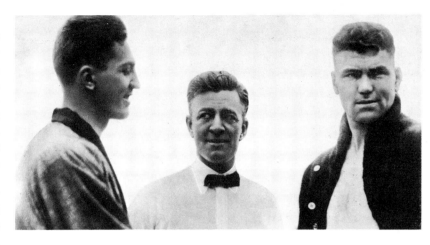

Yet Dempsey, who had practically bankrupted himself betting to win by a first round knock-out, should have collected his money. There had never been a first round like it in championship boxing history. Willard, who had nothing but his courage, was down seven times. The bedlam was so great that nobody heard the end of the first round and it was assumed that Jack had won by a knock-out.

But after Dempsey had left the ring, he had to be recalled, timekeeper Warren Barbour ruling that the round had ended when the count had reached nine. Willard was 37 at the time. Dempsey was only 24, and referee Ollie Pecord's decision to continue the mayhem for another two rounds must

Above 'Gorgeous Georges' Carpentier, the world light-heavyweight champion meets Jack Dempsey (right) before their bout in 1921.

Opposite Billy Miske down and out in the third round of his bout with Dempsey on 6 September 1920.

Below opposite Bill Brennan (left) and Jack Dempsey posing before their title fight on 14 December 1920 with Doc Kearns holding the towel. Brennan was knocked out in the 12th round.

Left Carpentier unable to beat the count in the fourth round with Dempsey standing over him. In the second round Carpentier broke his right thumb in a futile attempt to stop the champion.

Right and below
Dempsey (in white trunks) and Tommy Gibbons in the fight which bankrupted Shelby, Montana.

Opposite **Three pictures of the Dempsey-Firpo fight showing: Dempsey falling out of the ring; Dempsey climbing back in; Dempsey knocking out Firpo.**

have cost Willard a lifetime's pain and agony.

The full extent of Dempsey's amazing three minutes can be accurately gauged from these dramatic facts. Never in his life had Willard hit the canvas until Dempsey had put him there—and it was seven times in three minutes remember. Inside two minutes there was blood dripping from both Willard's eyes and also his nose.

The only reason Dempsey didn't stop it in the second round was that through a mixture of eagerness and inexperience he'd exhausted himself in the first round. Nevertheless, while Willard continued to exhibit a brand of courage rarely seen inside a boxing ring, Dempsey knocked two of Willard's front teeth onto the floor of the ring.

In the third round the brave Jess actually landed some punches on Jack, but the punishment, perhaps torture is the better word, went on.

At the start of what should have been the fourth round, the towel came floating in from Willard's corner. Enough was more than enough. Willard was unable to leave the ring without assistance. Later, they found that a cheekbone had been fractured in several places. Yet after that murderous first round, Willard had refused to go down again!

Willard could never see eye to eye with Jack. He always rejected the handshake of friendship believing that Dempsey had bolts in his hands before the tapes went on. Kearns, whose relationship with Dempsey was strictly business, alleged in a magazine article published after his death that plaster of paris was used inside Dempsey's gloves.

Later, one of Dempsey's seconds was to say that he bound Dempsey's hands with a kind of tape that stiffened when gloves went over them. But all the arguing didn't alter the fact that the Manassa Mauler was the new world champion.

Two minor title skirmishes followed in 1920, and then in July 1921 came boxing's first million dollar fight . . . Dempsey's battle with Georges Carpentier in New Jersey. This was the fight that put boxing on the high society pinnacle and though the Frenchman was a character in his own right, it was really Dempsey who put it there!

In the meantime, Jack had been in Hollywood, making films for big money, which he and Doc Kearns spent, and not risking his good looks.

Rickard's financial success at Toledo had laid the pattern for the future. For the Carpentier fight, the promoter again built another stadium, this one at Boyle's Thirty Acre field in Jersey City, and for once in his life the calculating Kearns, master manipulator, was outsmarted.

Rickard offered Kearns a percentage. At first, Doc agreed. Then he thought it over and changed his mind. Only a straight fee would do. The sum of 300,000 dollars was settled on. Carpentier's manager Marcel Desçamps was happy enough to settle for 200,000 dollars.

So Rickard's main commitment was half a million. But the gambler had done the right thing again. He'd backed a cert. And perhaps it was the feelings against Dempsey that were responsible. Jack was respected as a fighter, but there was no show of public affection. Boyle's field bulged with 91,000 people, more than most hoping that Georges Carpentier, handsome soldier hero of the war Dempsey hadn't fought in, would manage to get his famed right fist on the end of Dempsey's chin. It was a vain hope. Carpentier, a charmer with a fine boxing style that might have been acquired in an academy of sweet science, just hadn't got the poundage.

Dempsey and Kearns knew that. They

reckoned they were heading for a one-sided contest. And they were right. They thought the public would see it that way, too. That's why Kearns went for the lump sum and spurned the percentage offer.

But when Rickard and his associates counted the loot after Carpentier had been taken to the cleaners inside four rounds the take was 1,789,238 dollars, leaving them more than a million dollars to play with after Dempsey and Carpentier had been paid off.

It was the biggest triumph of Rickard's promoting lifetime. It made boxing respectable in the States. Among the Jersey City audience were several members of new president Warren Harding's cabinet, John D. Rockfeller, Henry Ford and Al Jolson. Jolson was different. He was the only person there wearing a bandage round his chin. It was a heavy price to pay for going a few rounds with Dempsey for publicity purposes a few days before.

Apart from the money, Carpentier had every reason for wishing he was on Jolson's side of the ropes. He'd had a look at Dempsey in the first round, decided in the second he could let that famed right hand go, and he did. It caught Dempsey flush on the jaw, and the Manassa Mauler stayed upright. What's more, the overriding emotion was anger. And Carpentier must have known then that he was for it.

Eventually, Dempsey saw the opening he'd been waiting for. In went that little old left hook, and Carpentier was down for nine. He got up and reeled into the path of a right that might have been fired from a cannon, and didn't get up again.

That was Dempsey's only fight in 1921. The following year was given over to exhibitions and high living. And by the summer of 1923 Dempsey's coffers needed replenishing and the great American public wanted to see the champion in action with his title at stake.

Left In their return match Dempsey (left) floors Tunney for the famous long count.

Opposite Firpo counted out against Jack Dempsey.

Below opposite Tunney (right) sends a left to Dempsey's head in his successful challenge for the title.

Below The referee pulls Dempsey away from the prostrate Tunney.

37

Then came the one straight out of a fiction writer's brain. Only it was true. Tom Gibbons was the opponent, and the fight went to Shelby in Montana. The city wanted the action, and they got it, at a price that put 300,000 dollars into the Dempsey fighting funds.

But less than seven and a half thousand turned up. It was the big financial flop. The city went bankrupt and four of its banks went bust.

Gibbons, surprise, surprise, went the full 15 rounds. He was a clever fighter. And I often wonder what Dempsey's and Doc Kearns reactions would have been if the cleaned out citizens of Shelby had offered to Dempsey and Kearns their city in part payment of the purse!

I prefer the story of Kearns loading the money into mailbags in order to get out of town fast!

Joking apart, 300,000 dollars was nice pickings, that's all. Kearns and Dempsey had another million dollar gate coming two months later in September 1923 against Luis Firpo who did one of the most gro-tesque impersonations of a human yo-yo in ring history.

Perhaps this was the fight in which Dempsey reached his greatest peak. For Luis Firpo was no freak. He stood 6ft. 2½in. and there was no spare flesh on him. He was all athlete, not a fighting gimmick.

Yet in three minutes and fifty seven seconds of so-called fighting Firpo hit the deck nine times. And should have won the contest had the rules been strictly adhered to. Near the end of the first round, when Firpo hardly knew where he was, he got up yet again and a haymaker of a right tumbled Dempsey through the ropes for him to land in the Press seats.

Now the rules say that if a boxer receives assistance back into the ring he should be disqualified. But with a flattened reporter and a concertinaed typewriter left in his wake Dempsey got the benefit of the doubt. Perhaps the referee, like everybody else in New York's Polo Grounds, was so bemused by the events of the preceding three minutes.

Because it had all started with Firpo

putting Dempsey on the canvas! Not long enough for a count to begin, it's true. But . . .!

Jack didn't hang about in the second round. A right landed on Firpo's jaw and all the lights went out! Dempsey was to have only one more fight as world champion, but that was three more years away – and to think that in these days we attack our champions for not fighting more often.

But those three years were significant. There were marriage troubles for Dempsey who, before he lost his title to Gene Tunney, had married screen star Estelle Taylor, and he was also continually in dispute with his manager Doc Kearns.

Yet, for boxing historians, the most momentous event of those three years was the one that never happened, a Dempsey fight with Harry Wills.

Wills' only obstacle to fame – who knows, perhaps immortality as well – was his colour. He was black. But he came from Louisiana, had a tremendous record and had tried for years to force Dempsey into the same ring. But, remembering Jack Johnson, the Americans did not want to run the risk of another black world champion.

At one stage, in September 1924, the contest was on. The tickets had been printed, for Jersey City. But the whole business fell through. Jack's decision, or somebody else's, not to go along with the

bout so angered the New York State Athletic Commission that Dempsey was barred from fighting there.

Promoter Tex Rickard always reckoned that he received a broad hint from the Governor of New York State that a fight between mixed races would not be popular. It explains why New York boxing authorities wanted no part of a proposed Dempsey-Gene Tunney battle, and that's why it went to Philadelphia.

All Dempsey's title fights have their place in history. This one in 1926 brought boxing's biggest crowd, 120,757! History doesn't record whether they could all see. Presumably, most of them were grateful to be able to go through life saying that they were there and let their imagination do what their eyes couldn't.

One intriguing aspect of the Dempsey-Tunney match was that bottom of the bill when Dempsey clouted Carpentier was one Gene Tunney who got booed from the ring despite gaining the verdict. Tunney, three years younger than Dempsey and one of the brainiest guys who ever got involved in boxing, had been deliberately waiting for the older champion.

Now, in September 1926, Tunney reckoned the time was right. And it was.

The fight was decided over ten rounds, not the now normal 15. Tunney, cold and calculating, won eight of them and in the fourth was within seconds of knocking

Below **The count finally begins five seconds after the knock-down. The extra respite may have been crucial for Tunney.**

Above **Dempsey charges forward as Tunney rises on the count of nine.**

Dempsey out. The years of inactivity had made Dempsey soft. The reflexes had lost their elasticity and his punch was ponderous compared with lightning speed that felled Firpo and Carpentier.

Pouring rain didn't help Dempsey. But I don't suppose it did Tunney any favours, either.

After the fight it didn't need any of the world's great intellectuals to identify the loser. One side of Dempsey's face was black and blue. One eye, well it was somewhere beneath swollen flesh. His body was throbbing in places that had never felt pain before.

And from the beautiful Estelle, full of wifely concern, I suppose, came the question we all hate: 'What happened, champ?' Dempsey, who had lost practically everything except his sense of humour, replied: 'I guess I forgot to duck'.

Dempsey wanted a return. But naturally. He wanted his title back. Promoter Rickard wanted a return. Shrewd Tex didn't need a financial adviser to tell him when he was on to a good thing.

But there was a snag. First, Dempsey had

to become the undisputed challenger. That meant a battle with Jack Sharkey who had done everybody a favour except the redoubtable Harry Wills by removing that particular menace from the list of contenders.

So Sharkey, later to become world champion himself, stepped in with Dempsey at New York's Yankee Stadium. And staggered out of the ring knocked out in the seventh, yet another victim of Dempsey's sheer ruthlessness. Dempsey belted in a stomach punch which some ringsiders thought was maybe a shade low. One of the three men in the ring thought so, too—Sharkey. He turned his head away from Dempsey to protest to referee Jack O'Sullivan, and that was the end. Sharkey should have remembered that Dempsey punched first and asked his questions afterwards. And Sharkey never saw the punch that smashed him down and out.

There was some consolation. Sharkey had a piece of the fourth million-dollar gate, and the first for a non-title fight. But that was just for starters. When Tunney and Dempsey met for the second time, the take

Left **In his turn, Tunney knocks Dempsey down in the eighth round. Dempsey also beat the count, but lost on points.**

was more than two and a half million dollars – in 1927.

Dempsey didn't know it then, but that scrap at Soldier's Field, Chicago was to be his last competitive fight. If it hadn't been for the famous long count controversy, Dempsey might have kept his title and gone on, and on, and on.

The background to the fight is all-important – and it was another title contest over ten rounds, by the way.

It was agreed before the fight that the neutral corner rule was going to be used. This meant simply that when there was a knock-down the fellow who had slung the punch went off into the furthest neutral corner. That's where Jack went wrong.

The fight had gone largely the same way as the first. Tunney was doing all the scientific stuff, and Jack was waiting to get a big one in. It came in the seventh, and Tunney went down.

Old habits die hard, and maybe Jack, the title almost back within his grasp, forgot himself. He reverted to type, and stood over Tunney, waiting for him to get up. Referee Dave Barry waved Dempsey to the neutral corner. Jack didn't go. So Barry stopped the count, and only started it when Dempsey did eventually move away. Meanwhile, Tunney, who wasn't badly hurt, reclined against the bottom rope. By the time Tunney got up, he'd been down for 14 seconds. He always reckons he was in command of the situation, and could have got up at any time. Jack doesn't agree.

But it is beyond dispute that in the next round, Tunney was not only ducking and dancing like a good 'un, but put Dempsey down. This time, referee Barry pushed Tunney to the neutral corner. After ten rounds it was Tunney who won on points.

That was really the end of the big time for Jack. But he liked the high life, and in 1931 and 1932 he was enticed back into the ring for a series of exhibitions which earned him another small fortune. By now, his popularity was as high as the Empire State Building.

He boxed three exhibitions in 1940 at the age of 45. They still wanted to see the man whom most American boxing fans still call The Champ.

Dempsey magic lasts for ever.

41

Joe Louis

STRICTLY ON THE BOOK – no other world heavyweight champion never lost a fight– Rocky Marciano has an undisputed claim to be regarded as the greatest of all time. But that's a matter for argument. What is beyond argument is who is the most popular boxer of all time.

There can be only one fist raised in the air in answer to that one, and the fist belongs to Joe Louis. Even Jack Dempsey made a lot of enemies early in his career.

Joe Louis, to the best of my knowledge, only ever made one. That was German Max Schmeling who paid for it later by being sent back home from the United States on a stretcher after Joe had extracted terrible revenge for the only knock-out of his career, apart from the last fight with Rocky Marciano when he was far past his best.

Because Joe is Joe, and what he is, that enmity died. Joe's hard times and tax troubles are well known. Max, one of the great fighters of the 1930s when he was used as a political tool of the Nazis, has done very well in business in Germany in the last 20 years or so.

When Joe was in hospital a few years ago, one of his visitors was Max. And who was it who made a more than generous contribution to Joe's hospital expenses? Max, who so many years earlier had been hit so hard by an angry Louis that his scream of pain cut right across the noise of a 70,000 crowd in New York's Yankee Stadium.

Maybe the key to Joe's character is that basically he's too nice a guy to have a quarrel with anybody.

The only other time in his life when I imagine Joe ever felt hate was in a car factory in Detroit when he wanted to hang one on a foreman who had just hit his step-father.

Joe was born in Alabama, but when young his stepfather had brought the joint family of 13 children to Detroit where work was supposed to be more plentiful. Joe had left school and had been working in the car factory for 12 months. He'd got a superb physique and had been doing the work of three men. So his stepfather thought it was time young Joe had a raise.

The foreman didn't agree. He landed a punch on the negro's head, knocking him senseless. Upwards of half a century of boxers must reckon now that that foreman has a lot to answer for.

Joe was restrained from hitting him. A priest explained that there was only one place where a negro can hit a white man without risking being lynched. And that was in the ring!

Left **Joe Louis (left) punches Tami Mauriello off his feet in their fight on 18 September 1946. Mauriello lasted less than a round.**

43

Joe became a boxer. But apart from those two minutes and four seconds of the first round against Schmeling, he never took his feelings into the ring with him.

Joe hasn't got a lot to say now. In his fighting days he must have been a reporter's nightmare. It was Yep, Nope and two fists. But he became, to use the phrase he really hates, a living legend. Joe did everything right, everything proper. He had to. Otherwise, he would never have got near the world title.

The United States of America didn't want another black champion. Jack Johnson's behaviour had appalled the whites. When he 'sold' the crown in 1915, the fight faction in the States made up their minds that there was never going to be a black champion again.

So right through the line of Jess Willard, Jack Dempsey, Gene Tunney, Max Schmeling, Jack Sharkey, Primo Carnera, Max Baer and James J. Braddock, the title had been kept white. But Joe Louis was good. Very good. There was no way, providing his

Above **Joe Louis delivers a perfect left jab to the body of former champion Primo Carnera.**

Right **Carnera (right) takes evading action later in the fight. Louis won by a knock-out in the sixth round.**

Above opposite **Former champion Max Baer counted out in the fourth round.**

Opposite **Max Schmeling (left) on his way to victory in his fight against Louis on 19 June 1936.**

conduct was impeccable, that he could be denied a shot at the title. Any slip on Joe's part and it could have been used as an excuse to bar him.

That's why Joe, throughout his life, has been very careful to keep out of racial issues, either way. He's been known to remonstrate with his own people when they've been prejudiced against whites as well as the other way round.

Perhaps Joe's character gives the clue to his fighting style. If Ali was the most extravagant, expensive in method, using up all that energy, then Joe was surely the most economic.

He was a beautiful, compact mover who would save his energy until he needed to explode it. Or an opponent gave him the opening.

I used to love seeing his films. He had such a great left jab. It was almost English in tradition.

A good left jab and a right cross are punches straight out of the boxing text book, and when they can be followed by a

Above **Louis defeated for the first time when knocked out by Schmeling in the 12th.**

Right **Like Max Baer, former champion Jack Sharkey is knocked out by Louis, this time in the third round.**

left hook that can knock you dead and a short right that can also knock you dead the whole package adds up to some fighter. Almost as good as Joe Louis, you might say. Perhaps, unconsciously, that's where I got my enthusiasm for the left hook as a punch.

It was the punch that kept my bank manager happy, but Joe wasn't so lucky. Though his fists brought him a fortune, he was badly handled financially. He was always owing the United States government money in back taxes. That is the reason, and the only reason, why he doesn't share with Rocky Marciano and Gene Tunney the distinction of being the only champions to retire with the title.

Joe, in fact, did retire an undefeated champion. He knocked out Jersey Joe Walcott in the 11th round in June 1948 and nine months later, after boxing a string of exhibitions, announced that he was handing in his title.

But when the accountants had finished totting up the bills it was discovered that poor old Joe owed the country more than a million dollars. That was why he was dragged out of retirement, tempted by the purse, to take on Ezzard Charles and be outpointed in September 1950. And why, 12 months later, he allowed himself to be used as cannon-fodder to the punching power of the fast-rising Rocky Marciano.

It wasn't good watching Joe in those fights. The memory of what he was was so much better. That's why I was never tempted back into the ring once I'd decided it was all over.

I had the chances. They dangled the cash to fight exhibitions, with Ali particularly. But what would that have proved? Once you've boxed as a pro, you never box again for fun. The amateur game is fine, but you never go back to it, and that is what exhibitions virtually are.

You start off just trying to display punches. You put on the style a bit, possibly get a little flash. Then one of you slips one in. It hurts. Human nature being what it is, you give him one back. And there you are, having a right old punch-up again, taking the pain and the punishment.

But what for? Not for peanuts, that's for sure. So I reckon, if you can't fight properly, then don't fight at all.

However, I never had Joe's money problems which were so bad in the 1950s that the interest rate became beyond Joe's means, never mind the little business of paying off some of the original debt. Then Joe turned to wrestling to earn some money, but a little bit of heart trouble stopped that.

Eventually, the tax department pulled out of their fight with America's favourite citizen. They waived the rest of the debt, which at that time had risen to more than a million dollars.

Now, there isn't a door in the entire United States that isn't open to Joe who spent some years welcoming the visitors to Caesar's Palace, Las Vegas. As I said, Joe's conversation, in terms of words, is strictly economy pack. But the guys who run the Palace didn't need Joe's command of words. His smile and his handshake were enough.

But behind all that shyness, Joe's talents spread to a surprising degree. He is quite musical. He plays the piano and the violin, and like another boxer I know quite well he is addicted to golf. But whether his handicap is better than mine, I wouldn't know.

And, he's a television addict. Joe's third wife Martha, who was a Los Angeles lawyer, bought a Spanish-style house with ten rooms. Then, for Joe, she installed eight television sets including one in the bathroom!

That's a bit of a contrast to the young Joe who turned professional at the age of 20 after winning a Golden Gloves championship.

Two Detroit businessmen, John Roxborough and Julian Black, were the men who managed Joe, and they were shrewd enough to get Jack Blackburn as trainer, shrewd because in his younger days negro Blackburn had been very handy with his fists. Later, the legendary New York promoter Mike Jacobs became involved in all Joe's big fights. But there was no doubt that the real guiding genius was Blackburn, after whom Joe named his daughter Jacqueline.

Joe didn't hang about. He won his first fight with a first round knock-out. His second lasted three rounds. His third lasted two. And it went on like that. In his first two years as a professional, Joe fought 26 times. He won 22 of those bouts by the knock-out route and won the other four on points. There might have been a shade of shrewd matchmaking among some of the earlier fights because, as I've said, that is what the boxing game is all about. But among the victims were former world champions Primo Carnera and Max Baer.

When Joe caught up with Carnera, the Brown Bomber had won 22 in a row. By now, Mike Jacobs was in on the act, and he reckoned it was time New York had its first look at Louis. Also, there was the little matter of just how good was Joe?

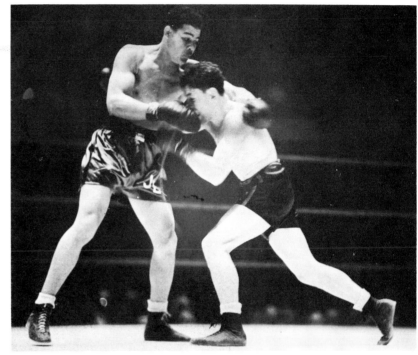

Three views of the fight between Bob Pastor and Joe Louis on 29 January 1937. Although both smaller and lighter, Pastor lasted the full ten rounds, but lost on points.

47

Above **Louis on the canvas in the first round of his challenge for James Braddock's heavyweight title on 22 June 1937.**

Right **Braddock hits the floor in the eighth round of his fight with Louis to lose his only title defence.**

Left Joe Louis raises his hand in triumph after defeating James Braddock to become world heavyweight champion. He was to hold the title for 12 years.

Below Former champion James Braddock leaving Comiskey Park, Chicago after his defeat by Joe Louis. His injuries included a severed artery and a closed eye.

Carnera, who joined the Italian Sniper Brigade to fight on the side of the Allies towards the end of the war, was a quarter of an inch under six and a half feet tall and weighed more than 18st. (252 pounds). And he was a vastly experienced 28 years old.

Joe Louis was only just over 21, an inch and a half over six feet and something like 60 pounds lighter.

Joe took his time. With the great physical difference between the two, there seemed no way how Joe, apparently dwarfed by the Italian, could ever knock him out. But gradually the accuracy of Joe's punching took its toll of the Italian's strength.

As Carnera got slower and slower Joe increased the power of his punches. It must have been something like the sinking of the *Titanic*. Suddenly, Carnera went. It was all over in the sixth round. Carnera had been knocked out for only the second time in his career. Max Baer had been the first to do it when he took Carnera's crown – and he'd taken twelve rounds! Joe has admitted since that against Carnera he delivered some of the hardest punches of his career. Lord knows what they would have done to a fighter even Louis' own size let alone one smaller.

New York wanted more. So, three months

Below **Tommy Farr.**

later, Joe was back in New York again, this time against Max Baer.

Now Max, a former world champion remember, was a great clown. He pulled many a trick, humorous and otherwise. But not even Max Baer would have gone into the ring with a one-time world champ two hours after getting married. But that's what Joe did.

Maybe Joe didn't rate Max. Certainly Joe's honeymoon with Marva, a secretary from Chicago, was in less danger than Max Baer. Maybe Joe was just a little impatient. By the third round Max was sprawled on the canvas, still trying to play-act by

waving from the floor after a left hook had thudded into his face.

In the next round, Joe hit him with a right hook. This time, Baer's arms didn't move. Neither did any other part of his body. Whether Joe ever invited Max to the wedding celebrations, I don't know, but what's for sure is that playboy Max didn't delay them for very long.

There were just two more fights to take Joe's winning streak to 27 in a row since turning pro and then they decided it was time for the big battle with Max Schmeling.

Whether Joe was really ready for it or whether it was the call of the cash that just

couldn't be resisted has been a big boxing argument ever since. What is significant is that Max, at 31, nine years older than Joe, had argued for a long time that the Brown Bomber wasn't quite as good a boxer as half his camp followers claimed.

Schmeling, probably because Adolf Hitler and his Nazis were leading with their chins at the time, never got the credit he deserved. But he always reckoned that though Joe might have been the greatest shuffler of all time there were gaps in his defence that could be exploited by some clever guy.

We know now who Max had in mind. 'Joe', he said, 'always carries his guard too low. He can be caught with a right swing'. The German also insisted that Joe's opponents had asked for half they'd got by allowing Joe to shuffle around waiting for the mistake.

Well, while they sat at the ringside that memorable New York night in June 1936 waiting for a Joe Louis knock-out victory to come up again like the re-run of an old Western on television, Max was sitting in the dressing-room with the think-tank in overdrive.

That's why, come the fourth round, Joe found out at last what it feels like to be smashed to the canvas. It was the first time

Above **Joe Louis won his second title defence in three rounds with a knock-out of Nathan Mann.**

Right and opposite **Two views of the knock-out of Nathan Mann by Joe Louis on 23 February 1938.**

in his professional career Joe had suffered the indignity of looking up at an opponent, and the punch that did it was the one that Schmeling had virtually nominated. It was the right swing.

Four rounds later, Schmeling, using the same punch, found the same target. Again Joe kissed the canvas. And in the 12th round, while the New Yorkers sat as stunned as if they were watching one of the biggest fight shocks of all time, which they were, Schmeling stalked Joe across the ring raining punches until again, that mighty right landed. And this time it was the last punch of the fight.

They patched Joe up, got him out of the stadium, and considered the future. James J. Braddock, one of the unsung champions, had got the world title. But how could they get Joe in the same ring as Braddock after the demolition job Schmeling had just done? Furthermore, the German was a former world champion and again was a serious contender.

Joe sat and brooded. Someday, he was going to catch up with Max, and there was going to be suffering on the agenda.

Meanwhile the negotiators negotiated. Joe knocked out former world champion Jack Sharkey in three rounds, and couldn't have done himself any favours because James J. Braddock, who died in 1974, would much rather have got in the ring with the older Max rather than risk a confrontation with Louis, who was back to complete assurance when he sorted out Sharkey only a month after taking that pasting from Schmeling.

Six more fights, all won, five of them by knock-outs, proved that Schmeling had done nothing to damage Joe's confidence. But the same problem remained. James J. Braddock's handlers didn't want to know Joe at any price. Well, nearly any price.

Braddock was managed by a clever character named Joe Gould. He knew that if ever he let James J. in the same ring as Joe Louis there was only going to be one loser. Or two if you count Braddock's manager as well.

So Gould, who would have made the characters in charge of the United States gold reserves at Fort Knox look like financial novices, did a deal which gave

Braddock a percentage of all the money Louis was going to make from title defences in the event of Joe beating James J.

Joe's subsequent 'bum of the month' campaign, then, could have delighted nobody more than Braddock. All that money coming in without sticking your neck out, literally.

It could have been Braddock and manager Gould who coined that phrase about laughing all the way to the bank.

On the night of 22 June 1937, in Chicago, Joe knocked out Braddock in eight rounds and the title was his. His reaction was immediate and predictable. 'Get me Schmeling.'

But, before Schmeling would be tempted into the ring, and straight out of it, came Joe's classic contest with Britain's Tommy Farr, a miner from Tonypandy who went the distance with Louis.

Joe was only keeping in shape for Schmeling he thought. But Farr gave him a terrific contest. He went all the way, fought better than he had ever done before and after, and made himself a national hero for the rest of his life. Joe reckons it was one

Left **Louis stands over challenger Harry Thomas after flooring him for the last of five times in the fifth round.**

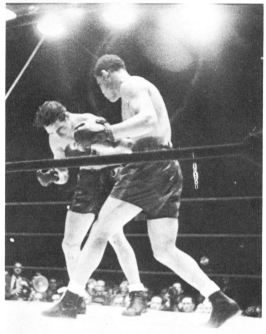

Above **A battered Max Schmeling hangs on the ropes in his second bout with Louis.**

Right **Schmeling under attack from Louis in their return match which lasted only one round.**

of the hardest fights he ever had, and, yes there was some booing at the verdict even from the ringside itself. It suggested that Joe was lucky to get the verdict.

That's a legend that has been built upon over the years, but now the time has come to nail it. Tommy himself says that the verdict went the right way.

Mind you, with typical American sharpness, they didn't do Tommy any favours. They called him from the dressing room 20 minutes before the fight was due to start, and then made him sit through a preliminary bout. It didn't work. Tommy said later that it merely made him angry. So he gave the New Yorkers a sight they didn't often see, an opponent going straight across the ring and belting into the world heavyweight champion. Unfortunately for Tommy he'd cut his eye in training a few days before and the story had got out. Louis found the cut under Tommy's right eye, and that was the target. After seven rounds there seemed no circumstances, short of a miracle, in which Farr could survive.

Joe was right in the mood. No mercy. He hit that cut again and again. Tommy should have gone. But he didn't. All those years of experience, all those years of battling away in the Welsh boxing booths, they all paid off. Tommy kept his chin, with some sort of miraculous expertise, away from Louis' thundering gloves.

And while the champion, confused by his failure to pin Farr's shoulder blades to the canvas, wondered what was going not quite right, Farr was bouncing back and raising the weals on Joe's body.

Tommy had the lot. Almost. Great heart, huge stamina, guts, professionalism, courage. You name them, they were all there. Except . . . a big punch.

And that got Joe, forgive the pun, off the hook.

For years, there was a feeling around, particularly among those who don't know boxing like those of us in the game do, that Joe might have coasted. But I'd have hated to be the fella who'd suggest something like that to Joe. Because it's nonsense. And unfair to both fighters.

Shufflin' Joe never carried anyone in his life. For this reason. Like most boxers, and I include myself, we're too darned lazy if we're quite honest. So being lazy, and feeling pain like the next bloke does, where's the mileage in any boxer making a fight last longer than it need do?

I know there are exceptions, like when Ali was having his hate campaign with

Above **The knock-out of John Henry Lewis by Joe Louis in the first round of their fight on 25 January 1939.**

Left **A surprised Two-ton Tony Galento stands over Joe Louis who got up to end the fight in the fourth.**

Right **Four views of Bob Pastor's second match with Louis. Louis finally stopped him in the 11th after knocking him down several times.**

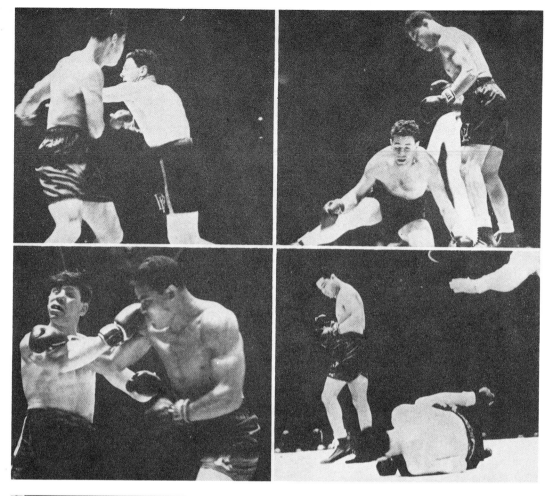

Right **The end of Arturo Godoy's second fight with Louis. The pictures show the right which ended the fight and the South American being restrained from continuing.**

56

Floyd Patterson, but generally, I'd sooner have carried a sack of coals round a football field than carry a fight. It's less painful.

The suggestion is unfair to Tommy, too. Without any doubt it was one of the best fights Farr ever went through, if not the best.

So why take the credit away from him? I'll tell you this. The fighters haven't any doubts. Joe has said publicly, not just once but many times, that Tommy is one of the gamest opponents he ever traded gloves with.

Joe went on to have two more contests—they both ended in knock-out victories, of course—before the one everybody was waiting for, and none more eagerly than Joe. There wasn't any way they could keep Schmeling away from Joe any longer, and nobody wanted it any other way.

Joe had been world heavyweight champion for 12 months when Schmeling and he ducked between the ropes at New York's Yankee Stadium in June 1938. The German was now eight years older than when he first won the world crown, and at 33 years old probably he and Adolf Hitler, the German dictator, were among the few who thought he'd got a chance.

Hitler had given Schmeling his orders. He'd got to win, for the Third Reich. That would prove not only that whites were superior to blacks, but that German whites were superior to any other whites. Adolf might have known a lot about politics, but he didn't know much about boxing.

The adoration wasn't all that one-sided, though. Across the ring, in the other corner, Joe, who needed no motivation for this one, had been promised that he was fighting for the free world against the Nazi world.

With respect to a great President of the United States, Franklin Roosevelt was wasting his breath with that one. All Joe said was: 'I want my revenge'. And once he was inside the ropes, he couldn't even sit down and wait for the fight to start!

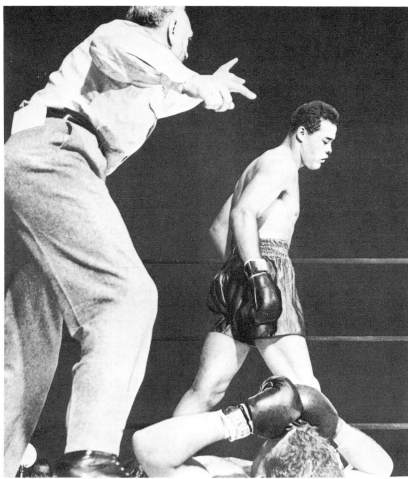

Above left **Billy Conn (left) in action against Joe Louis on 18 June 1941.**

Above **Louis knocks out Conn in the 13th after the challenger had attempted to trade blows.**

Left **Conn being counted out by Eddie Joseph in his match with Louis. The challenger was winning on points until he decided to slug it out.**

57

Joe was about to earn something like three thousand dollars a second–and remember, we're talking about 1938–but as far as he was concerned it could have been peanuts. Or even small change for peanuts.

The bell went and 70,000 fight fans settled back in their seats. Many of them reached inside their pockets for a cigar, thumbed their lighters or struck their matches–and missed the fight. At two minutes and four seconds of the first round, including the count, it was at that time the fastest world heavyweight championship victory on record.

The first two punches might have given Max the idea that he was standing underneath a collapsing skyscraper. They were? Left hooks, what else?

Then over went a right to the chin. And Max was down. Some of our moderns are supposed to punch rapidly, but with the aid of film they've since been able to calculate that nine rights went into Schmeling in the first minute. Twice more he went down, and that was enough for the German corner. The towel came floating in.

But they'd forgotten one thing. Under New York rules, that wasn't allowed. But the act persuaded the referee to have a closer look at Schmeling, and then he stopped the bout as the count reached eight.

As I've said earlier, Max squealed when one Louis blockbuster crashed against him. The next squeal came generally from Max's camp who protested that Schmeling had been fouled. They argued that most of Louis' punches had landed on Schmeling's kidneys. It was conveniently forgotten that Schmeling had turned into the ropes for shelter.

Schmeling was carted off to hospital. A few days later, the German was aboard a boat for home–still on a stretcher!

Joe, I suspect, has never been so angry in his life. Before the fight he was telling people that the German insults to his race were going to have to be paid back. And at least one journalist is prepared to swear Louis said he would get rid of Schmeling inside the first round and anybody who fancied it could go and bet with confidence.

That night of June 1938, Joe, then a month beyond his 24th birthday, was at his boxing peak. He probably never reached that peak again because at that time there weren't the boxers around to extend him and then, in the summer of 1942 when he was 28, the Army claimed him.

In those four years, was the famed 'Bum of the Month' campaign. As I've said before, some bums. There were men like John Henry Lewis, Tony Galento, Red Burman, Billy Conn, Max Baer's brother Buddy twice and many more. Joe gave them all a go. And they all failed. Arturo Godoy was the only one, along with Britain's Tommy Farr, who took Joe the full distance in a world title fight, before the Army outpointed Joe, for the time being.

When Joe went into uniform he'd had 57 fights. He'd lost only one of them, to Schmeling. And only seven more had gone the distance. The final bell and Joe were almost complete strangers. He had reigned for five years, perhaps not all that exceptional. But no other boxer in history had defended that title so often and so successfully.

Joe, in the 1940s, was revered by everybody except the United States tax officials and perhaps certain Germans. He was regarded as perfection, and by many good, shrewd judges as the best boxer of them all. Several folk whose opinion I respect very much held this view until Muhammad Ali came along, and now, like me, they refuse to separate them.

Opposite and left **Louis being tumbled out of the ring by Buddy Baer, Max Baer's brother, in their first fight on 23 May 1941. Louis won on a disqualification in the seventh.**

Below **In their second match in 1942 Buddy Baer lasted less than one round. This right cross finished the fight.**

Right A perfect left to Billy Conn's face in the second Louis-Conn fight. This time Conn lasted eight rounds.

Below The first Louis-Walcott fight. Here Walcott hits the canvas in the 13th round, but Louis was also put down twice and was lucky to win in a split decision.

There was perhaps only one period in his pre-Army spell when Joe looked in slight danger of losing the title. That was in the set-to with Billy Conn, the Pennsylvanian who was really not much more than a light-heavyweight. Conn, some 25 pounds lighter than Louis when they fought in 1941, gave the champion one of his toughest fights. And Joe was expecting just that. When they asked him, before he got into the ring with Conn, how it would go, Joe uttered the immortal words: 'They can run, but they can't hide'.

Well, Conn ran, or rather boxed his way out of trouble. For 13 rounds, Joe did his best to catch up with Conn. But never quite succeeded. He was a fair way behind on points, and realised that unless he produced something special, it was going to be Joe Louis, ex-world champ.

But, Joe was something special. And, as Conn, who allowed himself to get over-confident and start mixing it, stuck his neck out in a manner of speaking, he used it to move his jaw straight into the path of Joe's left hook. Immediately Joe, who had been looking sorry for himself, beamed. He knew it then. Conn didn't. But the end wasn't far away.

The famed right, carrying almost instant sleep, came hurtling through Conn's defences, and then a flurry of punches finished it just before the end of the 13th. Conn's feelings, when he came round to find that the referee and one of the two judges had him ahead on points, can be left to the imagination and Conn's temptation to cut his own throat.

Only once more was Joe to come as close as that to losing the world title and that was after he'd come out of the Army.

Conn had to be given the chance of a return fight, but this time lasted only eight rounds. Tami Mauriello tried his luck but

Left **Joe Louis (left) and Jersey Joe Walcott in their second fight on 25 June 1948. Louis knocked out Walcott in the 11th round in what was his last title defence.**

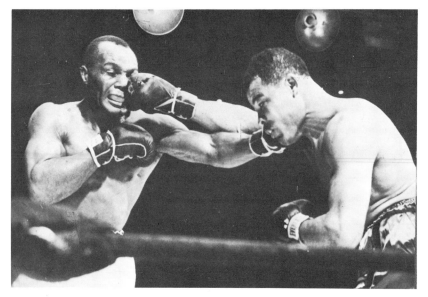

Top Louis (right) sends a right to Walcott's face and receives a left in return.

Above Joe Louis (right) batters Lee Savold to defeat in the former champion's seventh comeback fight.

Right Louis defeating Argentinean Cesar Brion (right) on points on 1 August 1951.

lasted less than a round. And then in December 1947, the ageless Jersey Joe Walcott finally got his chance.

By now, Joe was in his 33rd year and had been champion more than ten years. Jersey Joe was supposedly only five months older, but had been in and out of the rings since 1930.

Jersey Joe pleased everybody except the judges. He put a ring rusty Joe down twice, for two in the first round and seven in the fourth. Referee Ruby Goldstein, a most respected official, saw it seven rounds to Walcott and six to Louis with two even. One judge gave it to Louis by nine rounds to six, and the other made Louis the winner by eight rounds to six with one even.

But for the first time in his career, Joe knew what it is like to leave a ring to the sound of booing. If only Jersey Joe Walcott, the supreme craftsman, had gone forward more often than backwards.

The verdict was a bank manager's delight. There could only be one sequel, a return fight, and this went on six months later. This time, Joe was sharper. His reflexes had been quickened. It was just as well they had because for ten rounds Walcott, boxing very cleverly, reduced Joe to the ranks of mortals again.

It was Joe's 25th title defence and his last. And it looked like being his last in more ways than one until Walcott, again feeling that he had the contest going the way he was dictating, decided to stand up and swap punches. It was fatal, Joe could still hit harder and faster when he had a target within range. And Walcott subsided under a torrent of blows in the 11th round.

Joe had a look at the calendar, did his sums, confirmed that he had been around for 34 years and decided enough was enough. Too many people had been discovering that that chin, perhaps always slightly suspect, was not as firm as it was, and anyway, undefeated retirement sounded good. On 1 March 1949 he announced that the party was over.

How wrong can you get? By September 1950, scarcely 18 months later, the old champion was back in the ring, enticed there by the tax man. In the opposite corner was Ezzard Charles. Could Joe regain his old title? No. Ezzard cruised through to retain his crown, a comfortable points winner.

As always, Joe needed the money. So he said 'Yes' when they asked him to take on Rocky Marciano. When he was knocked out in the eighth there were tears at the ringside. . . .

Left Louis (left) in a clinch with Rocky Marciano during the third round of their fight on 26 October 1951.

Below Rocky Marciano (left) knocks Joe Louis out in the eighth. This was the old champion's last fight.

Rocky Marciano

I FIRMLY BELIEVE no future heavyweight champion of the world will ever surpass Rocky Marciano's record of 49 fights and 49 wins. He and Gene Tunney are the only two world champions to retire while they held the championship, but even Gene lost a fight or two on the way to the title.

There aren't as many fighters around now as there used to be so you don't need so many fights to get to the top. Then, when you get to the top, you don't fight more than once or twice a year. If you do, you're just keeping the taxman in business.

As far as the record books are concerned, Rocky's place is assured. His friends, and he had more than most in boxing, don't need the statistics. The memory of the man is enough.

Rocky died in August 1969, killed in a plane crash in Iowa with two friends. It was the day before his 46th birthday, and like most of boxing's all-time greats, his popularity increased as he grew older.

He never fought in Britain. As I've said his style, if that's the right word, of fighting would never have been tolerated in British rings. But that didn't stop his friends in Britain arranging a memorial service. I consider it an honour that I was asked to read the lesson, and it was certainly one of the most moving experiences of my life. Most of Britain's fighting fraternity were there including Don Cockell who took the pasting of a lifetime from Rocky, but was never heard to speak against the man.

I've heard Don's version of that fight, and there's one thing down on the record for certain—I'm glad I never fought Rocky! That doesn't make me unique. I'll bet most of the guys who did fight him regretted the encounter too.

There can't have been any other character in boxing remotely like Rocky. Because he probably had less skill than any other world champion, and he never really wanted to be a boxer anyway. And I know this for sure. When he first started considering retirement it didn't take him long to get out.

If you want it in one simple sentence it's this: he got out so that he could spend more time with his family. Though he was born in Brockton, Massachusetts, he was of Italian descent. Like all Italians, he had a very strong sense of family. He never lost it. Italians don't.

My wife Albina is Italian, so we belong to one of the Italian clubs in London. Every year, in the summer, we have a party for about a thousand people. Don't misunderstand me. Not in my back garden. It may

Left **Rocky Marciano sends Carmine Vingo to the floor in the second round of their bout on 30 December 1949. Vingo had already hit the canvas in the first round and was finally knocked out in the sixth.**

Above **Roland LaStarza being driven onto the ropes in the fifth round of his fight with Marciano on 24 March 1950. Despite the punishment, LaStarza lasted to the end to lose a split decision.**

have a small swimming pool, but I haven't done that well!

But we go out into the country taking huge marquees and our food and wine and music with us. I think I can appreciate more than most the reasoning behind Rocky's decision to quit at the top. He didn't like hurting people except in the course of duty as you might say. And he didn't like relatives and close friends seeing him get hurt. He didn't like it when his young daughter Maryanne visited his training camp, and his wife Barbara was anything but an enthusiastic visitor at the ringside.

In fact, if Rocky had listened to his mother Pasqualena he would never have been a boxer. She never wanted him to fight. After he'd served his time with the United States Army and come home to Brockton demobilised after the war, he went to New York to see that legendary boxing manager Al Weill.

By the time Rocky got back home, Mum was dead against it. She made his father Pierino tell Rocky he hadn't got to fight.

Or thought she had. Pierino admitted afterwards that he hadn't got the courage to go through with it.

Despite his mother's objection, Rocky fought. He reasoned that it was the only way he was ever going to be able to take his dad out of the drudgery of the shoe factory where he toiled all day with a mouthful of tacks and nails. It was that family loyalty which Rocky never lost.

Eventually, Pasqualena had to get used to the fact that her boy was in the fight game. She prayed that her son wouldn't get hurt. But that was in the early days. Later, she started praying that Rocky wouldn't hurt the others too much!

How and where did Rocky have his first fight? Well, I'm told that it was in Britain, during the war when he was helping to ferry vehicles over to Normandy. Rocky, who admitted that in those days he'd got weight in all the wrong places, was stationed in South Wales. One night, they were on the town. So were a bunch of aggressive Aussies who, as the evening wore

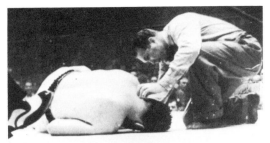

on, became less and less complimentary about the quality of American servicemen. Are you ahead of me? Somehow it was Rocky who got nominated to defend the honour of his mates, a Rocky who by heavyweight standards was no way among the tallest or the heaviest. But that Aussie's lights went clean out. When Rocky finished, the Aussie's head was nearer Australia than his feet.

So Rocky started his boxing in Army rings. As a boy, it was baseball he was interested in. Baseball's loss was boxing's gain.

And the man who gained particularly was Al Weill, one of the shrewdest boxing managers who ever lived. Al had managed three world champions, featherweight Joey Archibald, lightweight Lou Ambers and welterweight Marty Servo. He knew a good fighter when he saw one, and he certainly saw Rocky coming.

Al Weill put himself on 50 per cent of Rocky's earnings. It wasn't a beautiful friendship. How could it be when Rocky learned more about the financial side of the game? Later, much later, the friendship, never too strong, ended. I've heard it said that Weill was heartbroken at the split, but whatever the truth, they certainly made a lot of money for each other.

There was one big problem in the early days. Rocky couldn't box. He just didn't know the game's finer points. He had to be taught . . . taught very nearly the lot. But even Rocky himself never argued that science was his strong point. I think this might have had a lot to do with his decision to quit at the top. Rocky's limitations in other directions made it imperative that he do it all with his fists. And his physique.

Rocky was going to get caught more than most. And to take that sort of punishment, he'd got to be fitter than most. I'm talking about his later, big fights, of course. In his younger days he was putting opponents away so fast that he hardly broke sweat. You know, there was a spell of six weeks or so in the summer of 1948 when he reeled off five successive first round knock-outs! It

Right Joe Louis (left) receiving a right from Marciano in their bout on 26 October 1951.

Below Louis down in the eighth round. Marciano's defeat of the former champion made him a serious contender for a title match against Jersey Joe Walcott.

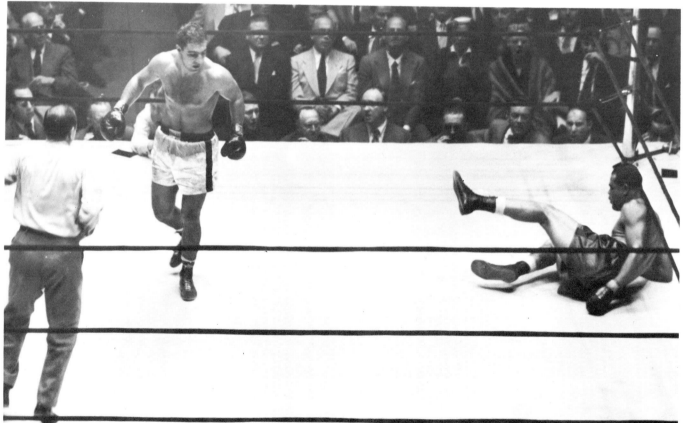

was great stuff from Rocky, but Weill's match-making wasn't so bad was it?

And I wouldn't knock Weill for that. Think about this boxing game for a minute or two. It's like no other. If you're not certain of winning a fight, or at least if you don't fancy yourself winning it, then why take it? It takes two to make a contract, and when you're coming up the ladder, you have a look at the rungs before putting your feet on them.

Nobody goes into paid boxing really for fun, do they? It's your profession, your living. Like anybody in any other walk of life, you want to make as much out of it as you can. Why knock the boxers?

Rocky defended his title six times between 1952 and 1956. The fights got harder because Rocky was getting older. I know he was only 32 when he told the world he'd had enough, but Rocky had taken a lot. And training was getting harder, too.

They should have built a monastery for Rocky. Before a fight he'd take to the hills, as often as not to Grossingers, the famous country club high in the Catskill mountains a hundred or so miles north of New York. And he'd go up there for three or four months before a fight.

I'm told he'd get very mean. Well, wouldn't you? I used to go away to prepare for a fight. You've got to. But I'd go for weeks, not months. And I always made a

Above **Rocky Marciano (left) and Bernie Reynolds. As usual Marciano was out-reached, but still knocked out Reynolds in the third round.**

point of being on the phone to my family every day.

Rocky used to say that fights got easier as you got older. They do. As long as you're still dodging the punches and the pain. But the training . . .! Rocky once said that when he defended his title against Ezzard Charles in 1954, the only time in his last 14 fights that he was taken the distance, he'd sparred 183 rounds and had done something like 800 miles of roadwork. 800 miles!

Rocky was so tough, it was almost

Left **Harry Matthews lasted just over a round against Marciano in Marciano's 36th knock-out victory.**

Above **Jersey Joe Walcott puts Marciano down in the first round of Marciano's bid for the title.**

Below **Marciano becomes champion by knocking out Walcott in the 13th.**

Brockton had ever seen. The Italian area of Brockton had gone mad years earlier when Primo Carnera had won the world title. For Rocky, it was going to be the whole of Brockton. Then he realised, when he was champion, that even as a world champion you're hardly left with that sort of money. Then there's the question of motives—other people's motives. Is it you they like, or is it your glory and your money? Boxing has far more hangers on in the United States than in Britain but one factor is the same the world over–the boxers take the pain and they take the pleasure.

Perhaps Rocky got out when he did because he cared too much. About his mother, for instance. Knowing how much she worried when he was in the ring, he had an arrangement with the family's medical man. Every time Rocky went into the ring, the medico would call at the family home, with his car. Then Pasqualena would be driven around until Rocky's fight was over.

Then Rocky used to tell the story of a very close friend who used to go to all the Marciano fights, even those in the early amateur days. During the first fight with Ezzard Charles, the one that went the distance, Rocky's friend died at the ringside. Rocky always thought that if he hadn't

impossible to hurt him. Most of his aches were heartaches. For instance, apart from the long separations from his family, Rocky admitted that being heavyweight champion of the world was nothing like he imagined it was going to be.

He had a dream that one day he would throw the biggest party his hometown of

Left Walcott is counted out in the return championship bout which lasted less than a round.

Below In their second clash, Rocky Marciano (left) hammers Roland LaStarza into submission in 11 rounds to retain his title.

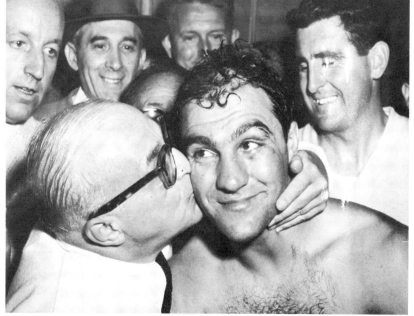

been boxing, that would never have happened.

Yet inside the ring that same Marciano could perform with murderous ferocity.

From the time he started his career in March 1947, Rocky ran up 16 successive knock-out victories. Then in the summer and the autumn of 1948, two boxers, Don Mogard and Ted Lowry, achieved some sort of distinction by being still on their feet after ten rounds with the Brockton Blockbuster. Early in 1950 Rocky outpointed Roland LaStarza, later to challenge him for the world title. Rocky was moving up the ladder–fast. The same Ted Lowry achieved unique status by becoming the only man to go the distance with Rocky twice. But although the opposition was getting stronger, nobody was stopping Rocky.

Now the names of Rocky's opponents began to have a familiar ring. Rex Layne was knocked out in six rounds. Freddie Beshore, who'd fought nearly all the best, lasted only four rounds.

Unhappily, for those of us who have a streak of sentiment – and that includes most of us – Joe Louis, making a comeback mainly for the benefit of the taxman, was enticed into the same ring as Rocky.

The old champ was 37. Rocky was in his physical prime at 28. Joe kept out of the way for half a dozen rounds. Then his legs started to give out. Rocky's punches went in faster and faster. It was obvious in the seventh what was going to happen. And in the eighth it did. Joe got off the canvas after a count of eight, took a number of minor punches, and then came the last punch that Joe ever took in a ring, a thundering right to the most respected jaw in boxing.

So it was only a matter of time before Rocky had to be given his chance for the world crown. It was 11 months later, after another string of knock-out victories, that Rocky stepped into the ring with Jersey Joe Walcott.

But already manager Al Weill had upset Rocky, starting a dispute that was never really patched up. On the last day of 1950, Rocky had married Barbara. At the reception, Weill called for silence and then made his speech, warning Barbara that boxing came first and she came second.

Straight after the fight with Louis, Rocky achieved another of his great ambitions. He was in the big money, so he hired his father.

At last, Rocky's father was able to quit that shoe factory, and it was a decision

Above **The British champion Don Cockell (left) attempted to take the world title on 16 May 1955, but was destroyed by Marciano's fierce punching.**

with Weill shouting to him to take a longer count. He roared in, swinging punches with hardly any control. Coolly, Walcott picked him off and sent him back to his corner with his left eye swollen.

Angry Marciano stormed out for the second round, arms flailing all over the place. Walcott had a seven inches advantage in reach, was two inches taller and 10lb. heavier. That would have made most boxers think a bit. But not Rocky.

It was a bloody fight. A gory fight. And by the 11th blood was running down from Rocky's right eye. When they came out for the 13th round, there was only one way Rocky could win. And he did.

Jersey Joe flicked his left glove for a

that was to have greater significance later. For his father was one of the most influential voices Rocky ever listened to.

Pop joined Rocky in his training camp. He helped him prepare for all the world title defences. He knew what Rocky was going through, keeping his body fit enough to take all the punishment. And he advised Rocky to quit, telling the champ that he was torturing his father as well as himself.

Rocky, later on, was offered more than a million dollars to do a Joe Louis, to make a comeback and fight Floyd Patterson. And Rocky turned it down. He blew a million out of the window!

Rocky was unbeaten in 42 fights when he stepped into that Philadelphia ring against Jersey Joe in 1952. Walcott was the oldest world champion of them all. Officially, he was supposed to be 37 when he won the title from Ezzard Charles, but he was believed to be nearer 42, and as far as I know he never denied it.

Not only had Rocky not been beaten when he went into that fight, he hadn't been knocked down. Ever.

So when the old man dumped Rocky on the seat of his pants in the first round for a count of three, Rocky was shocked. And so were his fans in Brockton who had bet watches, cars and even houses on Rocky's ability to take Walcott's title from him. But this was the fight that was to be absolutely typical Marciano, the fight that capsuled his whole career, if you like.

By 1952, Walcott had been around the rings some 30 years. That's as far as we all know because nobody has ever been able to lay his hands on Joe's ring record before 1930, and he always dodges those questions as adroitly as he used to duck punches.

Walcott knew it all. Rocky didn't. That's why he leapt up from the canvas at three

fraction of a second. He left his jaw exposed. And in crashed a right, one of the hardest punches that even Rocky Marciano ever threw. I don't suppose Walcott ever felt it. The world had a new champ, a champ who sat in the dressing room after the fight and had to have 14 stitches put into his face. But that was the rate of exchange when you traded punches like Rocky traded them. And Rocky was a good healer. He had to be!

After such a battle, there just had to be a return. The public wanted it, and they were ready to cough up. This time, instead of lasting 13 rounds, Jersey Joe went all of two minutes and 25 seconds–of the first round.

Marciano, the first white champion since the night Joe Louis toppled James J. Braddock back in 1937, had been feted to an extraordinary degree. His confidence had been built to unprecedented heights.

Jersey Joe was nearly eight months older, and a lot wiser than he had been when he first tangled with Rocky. It's impossible to believe that he actually looked forward to the fight. But he did have six children, and the memory of all that pain and anguish.

As I've said, Joe Louis never fought again after taking the full impact from Rocky. Jersey Joe Walcott never fought again, either.

They brought back Roland LaStarza next. A clever boxer, they thought he would

Left **Don Cockell was left hanging on the ropes in the ninth round when the referee stopped the fight.**

Above **World light-heavyweight champion Archie Moore (standing) was finally matched against Marciano on 21 September 1955 and in the second round put the champion on the canvas for only the second time in his career.**

going in with an opponent older than himself, though this time the difference was only two years, a lot less than Joe Louis and Jersey Joe were asked to give away.

In some ways it must have been like an action replay of Rocky's first fight with Jersey Joe. It was the only one of Rocky's seven title bouts to go the distance. He acquired the points verdict, and also 56 stitches in his face which Rocky obviously used to stop most of Ezzard's punches.

Rocky himself admitted that he didn't know how his nose stayed in one piece. He is on record too as saying that he was virtually in a knocked-out state for several days after the brawl.

But it wasn't Charles who won the fight, was it? Just like Jersey Joe, he was ahead early in the fight, but Rocky gradually, and painfully, wore him down. Just how hard could Rocky hit? I've heard the argument time and time again. We'll never know. But in this fight he broke a blood vessel in Charles's arm!

Three months later, Charles was in the same ring with Marciano again. But a lot more tentative this time, like Jersey Joe when he had his second confrontation with Rocky. Walcott, as we know, didn't last a round. Charles stayed in the firing line for nearly eight.

There were just two more pay-days for Marciano. The Cockell fight and a long-delayed meeting with the legendary Archie Moore, the light-heavyweight the big lads tried their best not to get involved with.

Cockell, by no means disgraced when failing to last the ninth round, got one thing out of the fight that nobody can ever take away from him. And that was this verdict from Rocky: 'I hit Don harder than I ever hit anyone'.

Rocky wasn't afraid of anybody. The fighter who could scare him just hadn't been born. So it wasn't Rocky's fault that Archie Moore, long-time world light-heavyweight title-holder, had had to mount an Ali-style campaign to get within punching distance of Marciano. Shades of Ali; Moore even offered a reward for anyone who could get him Marciano.

Al Weill must have thought he had waited long enough when the pair climbed into the ring in September 1955. Marciano was then 32. Moore was saying he was only 39 but convincing nobody least of all his mother who was laying it on the line that Archie was three years older than that.

Ageless Archie, as they used to call him, knew every trick in the book. I suspect he'd invented a few of them. And there was a

certainly give the crowd a longer fight than Jersey Joe Walcott had been able to do because he'd gone the distance with a younger Rocky three and a half years earlier. But I doubt whether anybody really gave him much of a chance of winning. Al Weill was too shrewd for that.

LaStarza did well for six rounds, but subsided to the full count in the 11th.

Then came the one that Weill couldn't avoid, a match with yet another former world champion, Ezzard Charles. This was the situation Ali used to exploit much later. If it's the fight the public want to see, then their cash is going to demand that it goes on. The only difference was that Ali used to contrive them with so-called hate campaigns like those against Joe Frazier and Sonny Liston.

Charles and Marciano, the public reasoned, had the makings of a great fight. And they were right. But again, Marciano was

story going around at the time that Rocky, who had been knocked down only once in his life, by Jersey Joe Walcott, had been toppled by a sparring partner while training for the Cockell clash.

Moore wasn't the kind of fighter who needed that sort of knowledge to boost his supreme confidence. But knowing that Rocky couldn't take punches like he used to wasn't going to do Moore any harm.

Bang! It happened in the second round, and there was Rocky, flat on his face. Moore argued afterwards that the referee took too much time rubbing the resin from Rocky's gloves. But I don't think there was ever any danger that Rocky would let Moore get away with such a blow to the champion's pride.

Like others before him, Moore had to learn to enjoy just the first part of the fight. By the end of six rounds Moore's handlers wanted the fight stopped. But he wouldn't

hear of it. By the end of eight rounds, only the bell had saved Moore. By the end of the ninth . . . well, that round never ended. Marciano's fists had done the job for the timekeeper and he was still unbeaten.

But that blow from Moore had signalled its own message to Marciano. Six months after taking it on the chin, Rocky announced his retirement. And stood by it.

He went into business, one of the most popular boxing figures of all time with his claim to immortality bolstered by being the only man to have knocked out four world champions, Louis, Walcott, Charles and Moore from the lower division.

Rocky wasn't all that sorry. Nobody was more pleased than his family, the family that had been increased by the arrival of a son by the time of that fateful plane crash.

Joe Louis, when he heard the news, said: 'Something's gone out of my life. Something's gone out of everyone's life'.

Above **Archie Moore was unable to beat the count after being knocked down by Marciano in the ninth. Moore himself had floored Marciano in the second (see opposite). This was Marciano's last fight.**

77

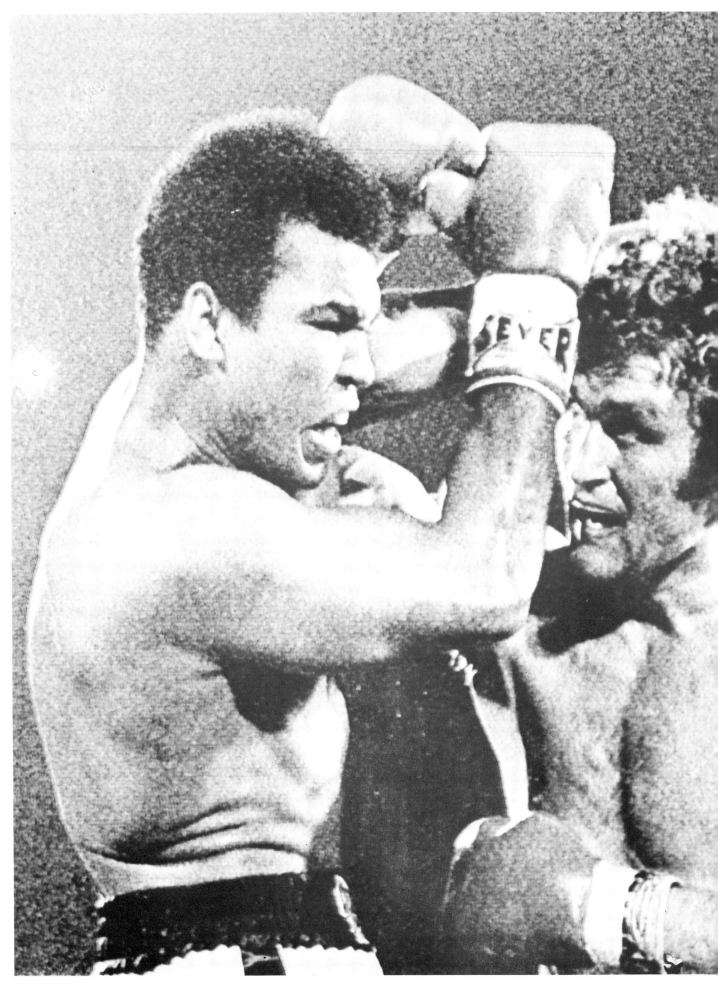

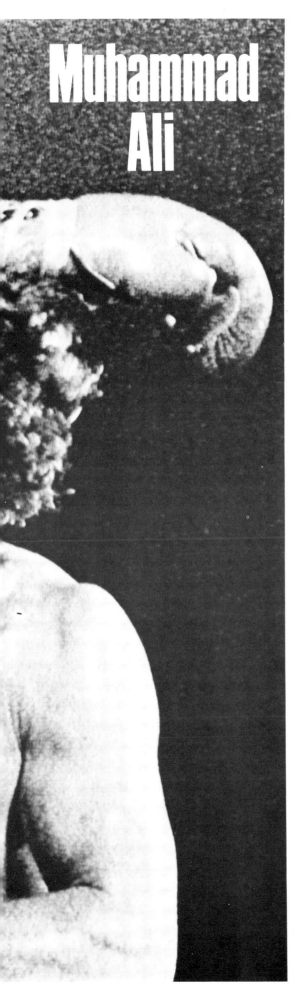

Muhammad Ali

HARD STREAK or not, I've seen Ali knocked out many a time. He's a push-over for children. That's the Jekyll and Hyde bit. As a negotiator, he's always had a sense, inbred I suppose, of his own value. I can't pay him a bigger compliment than to compare him with his manager Herbert Muhammad, and that fella's a financial genius who has been involved in more multi-million fights than anybody else in boxing history.

Whether Herbert has made Ali the greatest heavyweight of all time may be open to just a little doubt. But what is beyond dispute, is that Ali has earned more money from boxing than anybody else is likely to.

But the Louisville Lip, as he was known in his early days, is in the flyweight division where kids are concerned. Any one of them can handle him. This is the one area of his life, too, where the voice that has deafened the world is turned right off. You wouldn't think it possible that he could go through airports like Kennedy and Heathrow without half the population of the world knowing about it. But when he's on a mission for children he can.

I know. I've met him in London when very few people have known he was about at all. And he's been raising money for boys' clubs and charities organised by Britain's show business people.

If there is one story that sums it all up, it's this one: California doesn't like boxing. For years the game was banned there, and when Ali was having his slight disagreement with the United States government over the question of being drafted to fight in Vietnam, one of his bitterest opponents was Ronald Reagan, the one-time film star who was then governor of California.

Reagan's dislike of Ali was something he'd never bothered to conceal. But when Ali was training for a fight in Dublin a youngster broke through the watching crowd and asked for Ali's autograph. The answer, when Ali inquired his name, was: Michael Reagan. The boy admitted that the great Ronald Reagan was his father, and charmed Ali with a Black Power salute, in fun of course. Ali loved it.

One thing Ali hated was being introduced to any of his opponents' children before the fight. And if he knew, after a fight, that any children had been there to see the way he'd battered their father, he'd try and have a few words with them.

It's a strange side of Ali, and yet perhaps not so strange. Where he grew up, on the black side of Louisville in Kentucky, money

Left **Muhammad Ali (left) and European champion Joe Bugner in a non-title fight in 1973, which Ali won on points.**

Right **Muhammad Ali (World Champion 1964-1967 1974-1978).**

Above opposite **Ali taunting Ernie Terrell in their fight on 6 February 1967.**

Opposite below **Ali slams a right to the face of Floyd Patterson in their first match.**

Below **Ali with his daughter Maryum.**

didn't grow on trees. His father was a sign-writer, his mother had to work daylong cleaning and cooking in somebody else's house, and Cassius (Clay, as he then was) and his brother Rudy rarely rode together on the bus to school. Usually, there was the fare for only one of them. Ali admits that Cassius Marcellus Clay Snr became an expert at cutting cardboard in precisely the right shape to fit inside the worn-through soles of shoes.

Contrast that with the money the man's made for himself and his Black Muslim movement since and it becomes easier to understand him.

Mind you, that's easier said than done. When he comes over to Britain, we invariably meet. The promotion and publicity boys don't pass that one up, do they?

We get on well together. He's a very easy guy to talk to. But you don't get the chance to talk to him much on his own. He's natural. He's an extrovert. But he doesn't belong to himself.

He is never left alone. Invariably, there are one or two of his chums from the Black Muslims. And then the conversation has to get round to generalities. It's a pity.

I'd be the first to agree that Ali hasn't a nature that could be described as shy and retiring. But he has got a serious side that he doesn't let many of us see. I've always said that Ali regards two people as an audience, and once Ali's got an audience then he's away.

But very rarely on small talk. Ali has always got something he wants to say, either on race or religion, which is very serious, or some fight or project which he wants the world to hear about. And that's not always necessarily for real.

His temper is good. British television interviewer Michael Parkinson might not agree with me because he was once at the end of a ten-minute tirade during which Ali's mouth was a picture of perpetual motion. But Ali has always been in complete control of himself outside the ring.

Occasionally, inside the ring, it's different. Ernie Terrell found that out, as well as Floyd Patterson.

They both made the same mistake. They insisted on calling him Cassius Clay when he insisted that he'd changed it to Muhammad Ali. I must admit that I never saw the objection. First, a man's religion is surely his own affair, though it must be conceded that Ali has paraded his before the public with more fervour than most of us, and secondly boxing is full of fighters who have changed their names. Jersey Joe Walcott was Arnold Cream. Sugar Ray Robinson was Walker Smith. And Joe Louis and Rocky Marciano weren't exactly their real names.

Ali fought Ernie Terrell in February 1967. Before then, Ali had run up a string of knock-out and fight-stopped victories broken only by 15 rounds with the durable Canadian George Chuvalo. But Terrell, all 6ft. 6in. of him, was made to suffer for 15 pain-wracked rounds in which Ali punctuated almost every other punch with the question: 'What's my name?'.

When Ali was Clay, a boy of 14 with his ear slammed tight to a radio in 1956, Patterson became his hero by knocking out Archie Moore to become the youngest boxer to win the world heavyweight championship.

Above **Muhammad Ali (then Cassius Clay) wins the light-heavyweight gold medal in the 1960 Olympic Games.**

Ali relied mainly on two punches. Left jabs went in like pneumatic drills and thundering rights kept going in – but to the body, not the chin. The fight had to be stopped in the 12th round.

Terrell never won another fight in the big league. Patterson went on for a bit longer . . . long enough to come to Britain and knock me out in the fourth round with the best punch I ever took. It must have been, because I can hardly remember it!

Punches like that, instant killers, were perhaps the only part of the boxing armoury that Ali didn't possess. He had every talent in abundance, yet it is a myth that he was a natural boxer.

Sure, he loves the game. Sure, he loves to show off his skills. Sure, he liked to demonstrate a style of fighting that was all his own. But it didn't come as easily as all that.

Most of us are natural sportsmen in the general sense that we dabbled at most games before making boxing our No. 1. I played soccer, cricket, had a dabble at athletics and even rowed. Now, I play golf that gets me round 18 holes only about 20 shots worse than Jack Nicklaus.

But Ali? I've never heard of him doing anything else but box. There may be something of heredity in Ali's movements because his father was a dancer of exceptional style. But Ali himself says it was all laid down in two gyms in Louisville. He'd spend two hours in one, and then four hours in the other. And that was most evenings in his later schooldays.

It all started when he was no more than 12 years old, and apparently all he ever wanted to do was fight. So he fought, and fought, and fought. Boxing was his complete existence.

He was only 18, astonishingly young,

The controversy over Ali's conversion to the Black Muslims was still at its height when Patterson, seven years the senior of the two, tried to regain his old crown at Las Vegas. It was hardly the best preparation for the fight to have said, as he did, that he was going to bring the title back to America. It made Ali want to see Patterson's red blood – and he did!

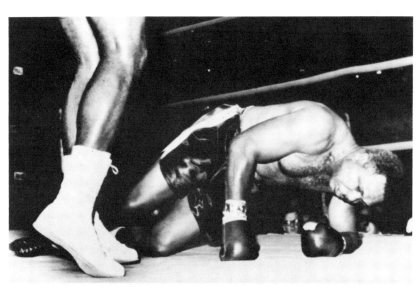

when he won the light heavyweight gold medal at the 1960 Olympics in Rome. Perhaps it wasn't so surprising. By that time he'd won 108 amateur fights, collected six Kentucky Golden Gloves titles, and the 1959 International Golden Gloves heavyweight crown.

Ali turned professional straight after Rome, his finances organised by a group of businessmen in Louisville. It wasn't a bad bit of business–for them! According to Ali 10 of them put in 1,000 dollars each and another got in free, for having the idea presumably and doing most of the work. By the time Ali changed to Herbert Muhammad's managership late in 1966, Ali's gross earnings from the ring were more than two and a quarter million dollars.

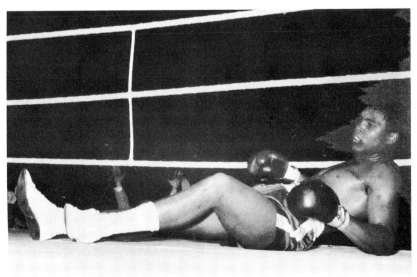

Above **Ali (left) stopped Henry Cooper in the fifth round as he predicted, because of Cooper's badly cut eye.**

Right and above opposite **Ex-champion Floyd Patterson (left in both pictures) was the next after Liston to attempt to take Ali's title. Ali taunted Patterson throughout his 12-round victory.**

I've got a source of quiet pride in that lot because apart from when he challenged Sonny Liston and won the world title from him Ali earned his biggest purse in the 1960s, around 450,000 dollars, when he defended his title against me in London. The first time he fought me he collected more than 55,000 dollars, so perhaps it's no wonder that he is so fond of Britain.

And Britain is very fond of him. Mind you, it wasn't always so. It wasn't when we had our first set-to at Wembley in 1963.

In those days Cassius, still on the way up, was just a shade noisy. It was when his campaigns to whip up the publicity for the fights were at their height. Nominating the round in which his opponent was going to go added up to sheer bombast, particularly in British eyes. This side of the Atlantic, that sort of thing isn't done, old boy.

Ali had told the world that I was going to fall in five. He was selling a good fight, but he wasn't exactly winning any popularity polls.

I trained for that fight in the south London suburbs. I'd get up early. I'd be on the road around quarter to four running, running and running. And I used to see these old ladies who'd be on their way to clean offices.

They'd shout: 'Go on, Henry lad, well done. Shut that big mouth's trap up'. They really had the needle with him.

Yet when I fought him the second time in 1966, it had all changed. London, at least, loves him. That's more than can be said in the United States where people, although they're not so vitriolic as they were, turned up and paid their money hoping to see him beaten.

It was like that when, still as Cassius Clay, he tangled with Sonny Liston at Miami Beach in 1964. Liston was champion then, and many experts thought he was a good champion. He had one of the heaviest punches in boxing history and many good boxers had felt it. Many of those experts argued that at 22 years of age, Clay was making his challenge too young. As he'd been in that Wembley ring with me all of eight months earlier, there was no way I could find myself agreeing with that.

But, in a pre-fight poll of 46 gentlemen of

85

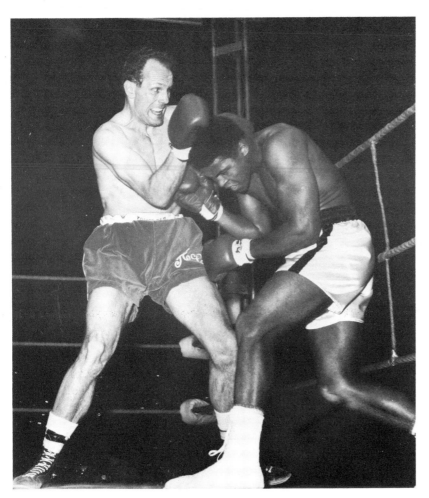

the media, all but three gave their prediction as a Liston win. Yet Willie Pastrano, the then world light-heavy titleholder and a boxer of beautiful science, was convinced that Clay was going to win. Those jockeys might be the world's worst racing tipsters, but we boxers do know something about our game!

For the first time the world got the full treatment from Clay at the weigh-in. Liston was known as the Ugly Bear. So Clay arrived with a jacket inscribed: Bear Huntin'. Pictures show him roaring insults at Liston. One eminent observer suggested that the fight be called off as Clay was obviously suffering from nervous exhaustion. He was even fined for misconduct.

Personally, I prefer Ali's version . . . that the whole thing was a carefully-planned and part-rehearsed put-up job. Because six months before the fight he bought a bus, and had his sign-writer father paint on the side legends proclaiming Clay as the world's greatest fighter and predicting that Liston would be beaten in eight rounds.

It was a campaign to whip up public interest to such a pitch that a fight between Liston and Clay became inevitable. And when it did, Clay was two rounds out with his prediction. Liston stayed on his stool

Above **In 1966 the second fight between Ali and Cooper took place. Ali won in six rounds.**

Right **Ali (right) knocks out Brian London in the third round.**

Above **Karl Milden-burger (right) struggles to his feet in the tenth round of his fight with Ali.**

Left Cleveland Williams (left) on his way down in the second round of his bout with Ali. He was saved by the bell, but the fight ended one round later (see over-leaf).

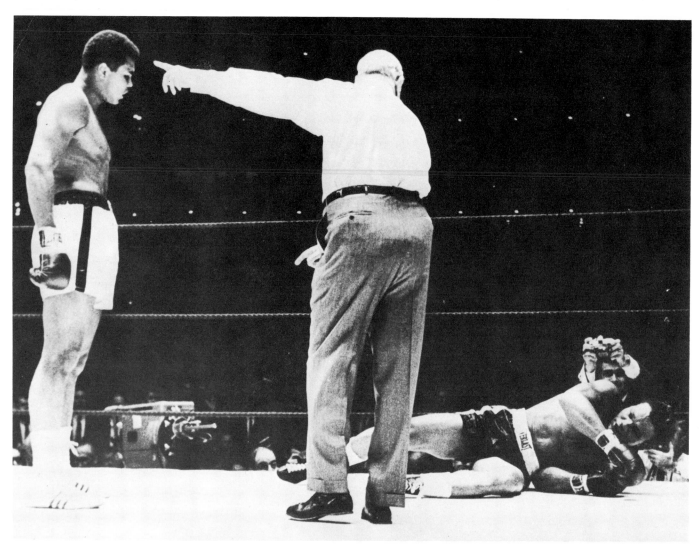

Above Ali watches as Cleveland Williams is counted out (see preceding page).

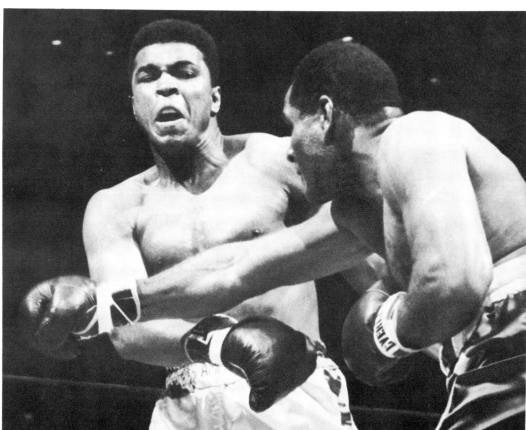

Right Zora Folley (right) was past his best when he challenged Ali in 1967 and lost in seven rounds.

unable to get up for the seventh round. His left shoulder had gone with tendon trouble and his eyes were cut. It was his first defeat in ten years, and Clay, using that name for the last time, was world heavyweight champion for the first time.

Within hours of becoming the most dangerous fighter in the world, Cassius Clay was no more. Muhammad Ali was born. While I repeat that any man's religion is his business and not mine, even Ali has conceded that the move did nothing for his popularity in the United States. All that has very little to do with Ali's boxing.

He stayed out of the ring for 15 months while they hammered out the financial details of the inevitable return with Liston. It was all about a return fight clause which a lot of people argue is not good for the game. I don't see how you can generalise. Each case has got to be treated on its merits. But if you've got to be a party to a return clause in order to get a crack at a world title, then you'd have to be a man of very high principles to refuse it. It's leaves that grow on trees. Money doesn't.

So eventually they climbed into the ring again, Ali and Liston, at Lewiston, Maine. Two minutes and twelve seconds after the first bell, it was all over. Liston had been knocked out inside one round in one of the most controversial title fights of all time.

The way Ali tells it, Liston was coming in off balance. Ali says he gave him a right to the side of the head. Liston went down, and never got up. Well, I've taken Ali's Sunday punches and there isn't one there that would knock me out in similar circumstances. But, all those folk who yelled that the fight was fixed were just yelling nonsense. Jack Johnson might have done so years ago, but in this day and age nobody gives up the world title.

The reason is so simple. There is no deal that could get anywhere near the amount of money to be picked up while you're champion.

I'm more inclined to go along with the people who reasoned that the bemused Liston was waiting for referee Jersey Joe Walcott, the former world heavyweight champion, to order Ali to a neutral corner while the count was going on.

Oddly, Walcott didn't do the count. The timekeeper did. And he, it seems was barely audible. Walcott watched Liston stagger off the canvas, some said to a count of 22, and in went Ali, punching away again without the formal 'box on' order.

Nobody now seemed to know what was going on. But when the greatest of all

Left **Ali in training and talking to his manager, Angelo Dundee.**

Below **Joe Frazier (left) forces Ali onto the ropes in their first fight. Frazier won on points to keep the title (see overleaf).**

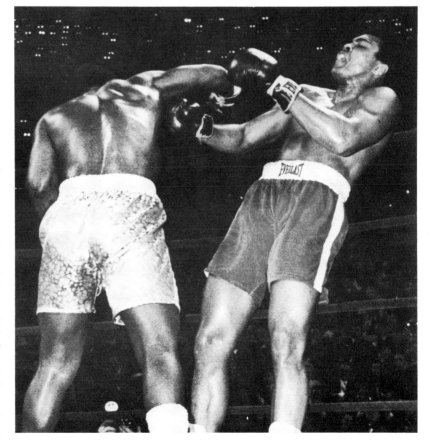

Right **Frazier downs Ali in the 15th round of their first fight, which Frazier won on points.**

boxing historians, Nat Fleischer, shouted from the ringside to Walcott that the fight was over, that the timekeeper's weak count had just not been heard, Walcott, ignoring the fact that Ali had not gone to a neutral corner, stepped in between the two men and declared Ali the winner.

What would have happened if circumstances had been normal is anybody's guess, but Liston never fought again at top level and always maintained that he was waiting to hear a count.

Why referee Walcott was not intoning the count with the timekeeper was never revealed. Subsequent film of the fight didn't prove anything either except that Ali's punch landed at one minute 42 seconds and that Walcott stopped the fight at two minutes 12 seconds.

Above **Jimmy Ellis (left) in trouble from an Ali attack. The fight ended soon after.**

Above opposite **George Chuvalo (left) covers up against Ali.**

Below opposite **Jerry Quarry (right) in trouble in the seventh round of this non-title fight.**

Right **A left jab to the head of Buster Mathis.**

Believe me, 30 seconds is half a minute, and in half a minute a hell of a lot of things can happen in a boxing ring.

So, who was going to cut Ali down to size? Former world champion Floyd Patterson was the next to have a go. But it was Patterson who got cut, and battered, and bruised in the gory battle that reflected little credit on Ali. As I've said, it was stopped in the 12th, and that was plenty long enough for it to go on.

Next in line was Ernie Terrell, but before they could get into the ring Ali had received that little message from his local draft board that was to cause him so much big trouble. He was told he could expect to be called up for the Vietnam war. He said he hadn't any quarrel with the Viet Cong, and was buried in public outrage.

No promoter would dare put him on in the United States with that amount of feeling running against him so Ali went abroad.

First he went to Toronto where brave George Chuvalo went the distance. But only Chuvalo will ever know the precise cost in pain. Then Ali came to London again, this time to Highbury Stadium, home of the famous Arsenal Football Club to give me a chance of becoming world champion. It was all set up for me, the most exciting night in British heavyweight boxing. I was doing well, feeling quite confident, boxing nicely within myself when . . . bang. My eyebrow, the left one, ripped open as if someone had taken a razor to it. The referee stopped it, rightly I suppose though I don't recall being very pleased about it.

I've heard Ali's knockers, and there's never likely to be a world shortage of them, argue that there were not so many good fighters around in his time. But there's one thing that they can never take away from him. He didn't duck any of us. We all, or nearly all, had our chance to put one, or two or three, on him.

After me, it was Brian London's turn. The Blackpool heavyweight went in with Ali at London's Earl's Court and lasted only half as long. Ali ruffled his whiskers in the third round and Brian wasn't able to beat the count.

Next stop for Ali, throwing his title into the ring for the fourth time in less than half a year, was Frankfurt. Karl Mildenburger, Germany's reigning European champion, kept going for 12 rounds before referee Teddy Waltham, then secretary of the British Boxing Board of Control, reckoned that Mildenburger, a southpaw who could be decidedly awkward, had taken enough punishment.

Later on I was to snatch back my old European title from Mildenburger when he was disqualified for using his head when the name of the game is supposed to be all about fists.

Meanwhile, back in the United States, the hate campaign was subsiding a little and after a year's absence from American rings he fought Cleveland Williams before inflicting that terrible punishment on Ernie Terrell. But within a few weeks of knocking out Zora Folley, one of only three fighters to k.o. me, Ali was knocked out himself – by the United States courts.

In April 1967, he blocked a punch with his chin by refusing to go into the Army. He was charged under American law and within a few weeks had been stripped of his world title by the boxing authorities.

Now whatever anybody wants to say about Ali's motives, nobody can question his courage. That decision kept him out of the ring for three and a half years and must have cost him quite a few million dollars in ring earnings.

Ali spent most of that time furthering the Black Muslim cause, but only in the United States. While all the appeals against his call-up were being held, he'd had his passport taken away from him.

Eventually he got a licence to fight in Georgia in 1968 where Jerry Quarry lasted

three rounds. But that was the least eventful part of Ali's comeback.

As I've said, Ali wasn't the most popular man in America and one night when he stepped out on the porch of the bungalow where he was training at least four shots whistled past his head.

For once, this was no Ali publicity stunt. Telephone threats followed warning Ali against stepping into the ring and resuming his fight career. And the police escort was increased.

It was all kept quiet and the fight went on. Ali was a winner again. He was on the way back. The story of the shooting didn't get out at the time. As I said, the man's courage is beyond question.

But soon there was another test of Ali's courage—in the ring this time. The first instalment of his great three-fight saga with Joe Frazier, who had become world champion, was one of the biggest fight occasions of all time. It could hardly be otherwise, could it, with both boxers being paid more than a million pounds?

At this stage of their careers, both Ali and Frazier were undefeated too. Anybody who was anybody had made the attempt to get into Madison Square Garden that night in March 1971. Television screened the contest to something like 50 different countries.

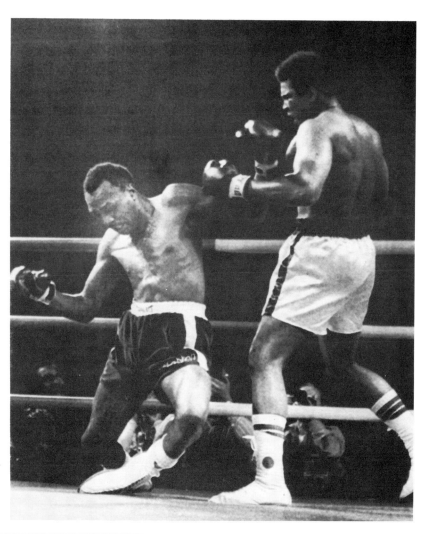

Above **Ali easily defeated light-heavyweight champion Bob Foster in eight rounds in 1972.**

Above opposite and below opposite **On 19 July 1972 Ali fought Al (Blue) Lewis in Dublin and won with a knock-out in the 11th. The lower picture shows Lewis down in the fifth round.**

Left **Joe Bugner (right) took Ali the distance in their non-title fight, but lost on points.**

Above **Ken Norton (left) and Ali in their first fight on 31 March 1973 which Norton won on points.**

Below **Norton (left) loses to Ali on a split points decision.**

And Ali, with only two fights in four years, was facing a Smokin' Joe who was probably then at the peak of his career.

Incredibly Ali took it all, even getting up off the floor in the last round after taking a count for only the third time in his life.

Frazier got the verdict, on points. Both boxers were taken to hospital, Ali for an x-ray on a suspected fractured jaw, and Frazier for general exhaustion. Ali left the hospital immediately the cameras confirmed that the non-stop jaw was still in one good piece. Frazier, depressed and having trouble with his kidneys, stayed there three weeks!

Next time they met, in January 1974, the ante had been raised to three million dollars each, figures that to a Joe Louis still haunted by the tax authorities must have been more painful than any punch the ex-world champion ever took.

By this time Frazier had lost his world title to George Foreman, and wanted it back. Ali had recovered from having his jaw broken by Ken Norton and you can imagine how he wanted his title back. But whether Frazier beat Ali or whether Ali got the better of Frazier there was still Foreman to roll over as well.

There was another question to answer. Ali's jaw. He was probably the only man in the world capable of fighting with a broken jaw for ten rounds but that's what he did against Norton who got a points verdict after 12 rounds. Ali had fought Norton again since and reversed the points verdict. He'd gone in with a guy named Rudi Lubbers and got another points win over 12 rounds.

But what we didn't know was what would happen when Frazier landed one of his tremendous blockbusters on Ali's jaw. If he could!

And anyway, Ali and Frazier had a grudging respect for each other. Mind you, they didn't spoil the box office by telling anybody about it for years afterwards.

They packed a few round the ringside at Madison Square Garden. But that was to provide some noise for the fighters. The total take, once closed-circuit and film rights had been calculated was a small matter of 25 million dollars. The big matter, for Ali, was the seventh round. Frazier got the old left hook working really well, and Ali's face took them nearly all, but then Ali cruised, if you could cruise against Frazier, through to a points win.

That evened the score with Smokin' Joe. Now the problem was to get Ali and Foreman into the same ring. That wasn't difficult. Because, at that time, the Bank of Zaire had got its lads on overtime printing money just to give it to Ali and Foreman. At least that's how it seemed to me when I heard that both of them were getting over five million bucks apiece!

The Ali camp had also let it be leaked to Foreman that the old man's legs were not so good as they were.

Well, we all remember what happened. Zaire were paying up to put the name of one of Africa's emergent nations on the world

Left The second fight between Joe Frazier (left) and Muhammad Ali took place on 28 January 1974 and was won on points by Ali.

Below Perspiration explodes from George Foreman's head after a right from Ali. Ali regained the heavyweight championship by a knock-out in the eighth (see overleaf).

map in letters that spelled Ali and they got their money's worth. Ali, on the morning of 30 October 1974 – they had to fight at 4 a.m. for worldwide telecasts – became world champion again after seven and a half years.

Put like that, it sounds simple, doesn't it. But Ali was then 32; he was giving Foreman seven years. The bookies made Ali 4-1 against, and nobody protested, or got killed in the rush to lay down their money.

Foreman was 6ft. 4in. and went in at 15st. 10lb. (220 pounds). He'd gone through Frazier in less than two rounds. Then he'd improved on that by knocking out Jose Roman of Puerto Rico in two minutes. Norton lasted two minutes into the second round.

All that made Foreman appear the most frightening man in the world. He'd had 40 fights and won 37 of them by the knock-out route. Also, he was angry. The fight had had to be postponed for five weeks while he

Above **Ali regains the title with a knock-out of George Foreman (left).**

Right and above opposite **Ali was downed in the ninth round of his battle with Chuck Wepner (right in upper picture), but recovered to stop him in the 15th.**

Below opposite **European champion Joe Bugner falls back from an Ali attack, but stayed on his feet to lose on points.**

96

recovered from cutting his right eye in
training, and that was five more weeks of
having to listen to Ali shouting the odds to
the world.

You can't blame Foreman for not being
pleased. After all, he'd cut Frazier and
Norton to ribbons, and they were the only
men to have beaten Ali.

There was only one way Foreman could
fight. So he came out throwing punches.

Why not? It hadn't been exactly unsuccessful as a tactic.

There's only one way Ali could fight. So
he came out dancing which isn't quite what
Foreman expected. Foreman's opponents
usually wanted to get on their bikes and
travel in the reverse direction.

Then came Ali's master-stroke. And at
the bottom of it was rooted the man's cold
courage. He stopped dancing. He went back

99

Right Ali (right) kept his title by winning his third fight with Norton on points.

Right Earnie Shavers walks away after downing Ali in the 14th. Ali recovered to win on points.

on the ropes and invited Foreman to hit him.

One of the first instructions that you get hammered into you, painfully, when you start boxing, is not to get caught on the ropes. And it wasn't how the fight had been planned.

Ali's corner panicked. They yelled at him to get off the ropes. But Ali was backing his brain and his boxing skill. He took most of Foreman's blows on his arms. And Foreman couldn't understand it. People didn't fight like that.

And Ali found the time to talk. Deliberately. Between throwing punches that missed and exhausted his energy Foreman was asked if that was the best he could do. Ali called him an amateur. Reminding Foreman that he was the champion, Ali requested that he show him something.

By the seventh, the man with the most powerful punch in the world, was gone – talked out of it. Confused out of it. Where there had once been power there weren't even wits. He came out for the eighth. Ali waited on the ropes, waited for the opening, and then struck. Foreman was k.o.'d.

Ali said, surprise, surprise: 'I'm a genius'. And at that moment there weren't many who would argue with him. Except Frazier.

With the score at 1-1, the third Ali-Frazier fight was a natural. It was only a matter of getting somebody to pay for it. Ali kept himself in business by defending the title against Chuck Wepner, Ron Lyle and Britain's Joe Bugner who went the distance with Ali in Kuala Lumpur in 1975.

Finally, it was staged in the Phillipines. Yes, it was the 'Thrilla in Manila'. And it

was the only fight in the history of boxing which carried a million dollar sidestake.

The match was made at six million dollars to Ali and more than two million for Frazier. They agreed that the loser gave the winner a million out of his own purse. And after it had finished, with Frazier stopped from coming out for the last round by his manager Eddie Futch, Ali was to admit: 'In the tenth I had this feeling that I was close to death'.

This time, Ali wasn't putting it on, any more than his collapse on the canvas, once he knew that the fight was over, was anything but genuine.

Genuine, too, was his reply to President Marcos of the Philippines who remembered the million dollar side bet. Ali said; 'Joe don't owe me nothing. We've paid all the dues we're ever going to pay each other'.

Whatever else Ali does in his life, I don't believe he can ever surpass those 41 rounds with Frazier.

Above **Leon Spinks sends a left to Ali's head in their match on 22 February 1978.**

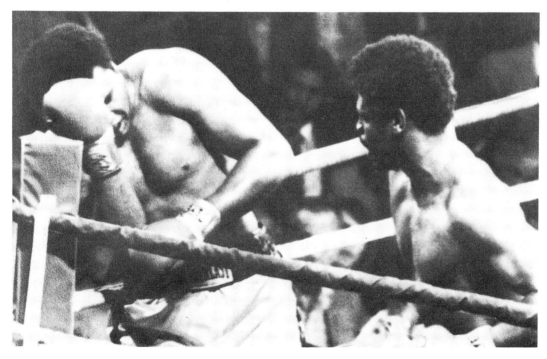

Left **In a surprise result, Leon Spinks (right) defeated Ali to become the new world champion.**

From Bare Knuckles to Dempsey

JOHN L. SULLIVAN, the Boston Strong Boy, didn't put a glove on in a title fight until September 1892. By then, he'd been heavyweight champion of the world for ten years and must have thought his manly sport was degenerating into a pouf's game. But it wasn't. It was just getting a little civilised.

When John L., the Champion of Champions to everybody who saw him fight, became top man in the world in 1882, he'd had to sign for a fight to the finish and put up 2,500 dollars in sidestake to get Irishman Paddy Ryan into the ring.

And it didn't take John L. long to get Ryan out of it. Just nine rounds, actually, with the help of bare knuckles and a few wrestling throws. For what was to become boxing when they made Sullivan and James J. Corbett put the gloves on for their title fight, was still prize fighting when the daunting John L. started putting his fists about.

They did wear gloves, of course. For exhibitions. But when a title was put at stake, then the gloves were off! Naturally.

They didn't fight so often in those days. It was six years before Sullivan defended his crown. Then he shot off to the privacy of Paris to engage Britain's Charlie Mitchell in secret, over a mere 39 rounds. It was decided that a draw would do sufficient honour to both sides, apart from allowing them all to get away before the police stumbled across them.

American police were much more involved. A certain Richard K. Fox, who was the owner of 'Police Gazette', had presented Jake Kilrain with a championship belt because Sullivan had consistently refused the fight. Well, being a man with something stronger than water in his veins most of the time, Sullivan decided the time had come to sort Kilrain out.

There was a side bet of 10,000 dollars at Richburg, Mississippi on that July day in 1889. The ring was 24 feet square, and the number of rounds a mere 75! They had been bare-knuckling each other for two hours and sixteen minutes before Kilrain decided that he couldn't go on. And that was the last of the no-gloves title fights.

I think it was appropriate that Sullivan should be there at the birth of boxing. For he'd sold the fight game to the American public and laid down a lot of the legends.

I don't know what they called Sullivan then, but now we'd call him an extrovert, and be on our guard. Between fights, Sullivan acted. Come to think of it, perhaps the difference between him and Ali is not all that great!

Left **Jess Willard (left) in a maul with Jack Johnson in their championship fight on 5 April 1915. Willard knocked out Johnson in the 26th round of 40-round fight after being out-boxed in the first half of the match.**

103

Above **Sullivan and Kilrain in the last of the bare-knuckle fights which was held on 8 July 1889. After 75 rounds Kilrain retired leaving Sullivan undisputed champion.**

Right **John L. Sullivan (World Champion 1882-1892).**

Far right **James J. Corbett (World Champion 1892-1897).**

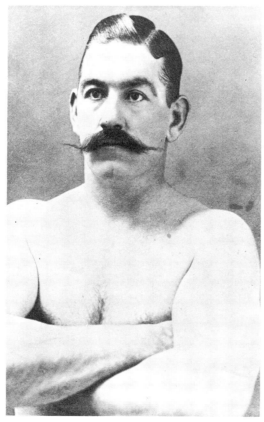

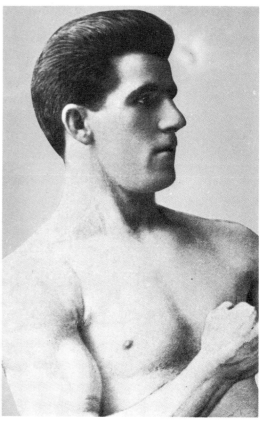

Far left A drawing of the title fight between Gentleman Jim Corbett (right) and Charlie Mitchell in 1894. In this first defence of the title he won from Sullivan, Gentleman Jim knocked Mitchell out in three rounds.

Left The British boxer Charlie Mitchell who unsuccessfully challenged Sullivan and Corbett for the heavyweight championship.

For three years before the Corbett fight, Sullivan had been bouncing round the United States playing in 'Honest Hearts and Willing Hands'. You'll have to take my word for it that it wasn't a tearjerker, but certainly Sullivan often turned it into one. He was one of the great drinkers of his time, a legend in his own whisky glass. Later on John L. travelled the length and breadth of America lecturing on the evils of drink. One Sullivan fight, with his opponent already in the ring, had just been postponed for the reason that the great man was indisposed.

Then in strode Sullivan, still fully dressed with diamond studs flashing, to make it perfectly obvious what the indisposition was. When the solid citizens of Boston decided to honour their hero they gave him a belt studded with 397 diamonds.

They could hardly do less for a man who announced on arrival in Britain that the person he most wanted to meet was the Prince of Wales whom he subsequently greeted with: 'How's your mother?'. I doubt if Queen Victoria was amused!

Sullivan's fight with Gentleman Jim Corbett went into the 21st round before Corbett, a bank clerk erudite enough to write a book called 'The Roar of the Crowd', knocked John L. out. It could easily be that Corbett, son of a Los Angeles livery stable owner, and Gene Tunney must rank as the two most scientific heavyweights.

Going on the stage was very definitely the vogue. Corbett followed Sullivan's example and toured in 'Gentleman Jack'. He stayed out of the ring for more than 12 months until goaded back by abuse from the same Charlie Mitchell who drew with Sullivan in Paris. Mitchell, not even remotely in the same class as Corbett as a stylist, was stopped in the third round painfully.

Corbett would have liked to have got out of the game neatly then, but British-born Bob Fitzsimmons whose family had left Helston, Cornwall, for New Zealand when he was a child, was making rude noises in Corbett's direction. They built a stadium in Carson City specially for the fight. Corbett's left and right coated Fitzsimmons

with blood by the eighth, but in the 14th the Englishman delivered the first blow to the solar plexus.

The year was 1897. It was the first time the punch had been demonstrated. And it paralysed Corbett. He couldn't move. Not until after the count, when he tore across to get at Fitzsimmons in anger and frustration. 'Pompadour' Jim had to be restrained by seconds and officials inside the ring.

Three years on, Corbett almost got his old title back when he took on James J. Jeffries. For 22 rounds, Corbett kept the big puncher away. Then Jeffries proved that despite all the science, a gap of nine years is too much. Corbett had one more attempt to hold Jeffries, in 1903. But the years had taken their toll and Corbett's last fight lasted only ten rounds. He made the stage his career after that.

Fitzsimmons had already learned the same lesson the same hard way. He was champion for just over two years and then in his first defence, against James J. Jeffries at Coney Island in 1899, he tried to give away 13 years and got clobbered in the 11th round.

Fitzsimmons was one of the lightest of the heavyweights. He won the world middleweight title by beating Jack Dempsey the Nonpareil by knocking him out in 13 rounds in 1891. It was six years later when Ruby Robert, as Fitz was nicknamed, took Corbett's heavyweight title. And in 1903 he completed the treble, though he never held more than one title at a time, by outpointing George Gardner over 20 rounds at San Francisco in 1903 for the world light-heavyweight title.

Like Sullivan and Corbett, Fitzsimmons

On 21 February 1896 at Langtry, Texas, Bob Fitzsimmons defeated Bob Maher in one round to become Corbett's main challenger. The pictures *above* and *right* show a drawing of the fight and the actual event.

Left **Bob Fitzsimmons (left) in action against defending champion James J. Corbett at Carson City, Nevada on 17 March 1897. Fitzsimmons won in the 12th round with a blow to Corbett's solar plexus.**

went on the stage. But he found it far more difficult to give the game up. He had his last fight at the age of 52.

James J. Jeffries was one of the ring's indestructibles. Known simply as the Boilermaker, he was a mixture of Scotch, Dutch and American. He came originally from Ohio, but made his home in California. He was 6ft. 2in. and weighed nearly 16st. (224 pounds) – and he was only 16 at the time.

Apart from having a punch that might have knocked a horse out, Jeffries' greatest asset was sheer patience. Many's the time he would let blows bounce off him, waiting, just waiting to get that straight left in. That's how he accounted for Fitzsimmons. He crouched and kept out of the way of Fitzsimmons' own left, which was more than just an adornment. Jeffries knew that his chance would come. And it did.

Left **Bob Fitzsimmons (World Champion 1897-1899).**

107

Above **James J. Jeffries (standing right) and Bob Fitzsimmons (standing left) sign for a return match which Jeffries won in the eighth to retain his title.**

Right **James J. Jeffries (left) and Bob Fitzsimmons shake hands before their title fight on 9 June 1899. Jeffries knocked out the champion in the 11th.**

Fitzsimmons found it difficult to stop boxing. *Left* he poses before losing his light-heavyweight title to Jack O'Brien in 1905 and *below* fights in vain for the Australian heavyweight championship when aged 47.

Eventually, though, Jeffries did run out of patience. He was so good that he ran out of opponents. He'd outpointed Tom Sharkey over 25, he'd taken care of Jim Corbett with that 23rd round knock out, he'd put Fitzsimmons away for a second time in eight rounds, he'd had his third set of fisticuffs with James J. Corbett, and he'd knocked Jack Munroe out in two rounds. He called it a day.

He had fewer contests than any other world heavyweight champion under Queensberry Rules, and it took him only 11 fights to become the world champ. When he met Sharkey, the unfortunate loser ended up in hospital nursing broken ribs. Perhaps it wasn't so surprising that Jeffries ran out of opponents.

Boxing wondered where the next champion was coming from. But Jeffries didn't.

With commendable arrogance, and the world loves a man of decision doesn't it, Jeffries nominated Marvin Hart and Jack Root to fight for his old title. Jeffries even deigned to referee it, which was a nice touch. But any possible embarrassment was foiled when Hart produced his own referee, a knock-out punch in the 12th round.

That arrangement might have suited Jeffries. I've no doubt it suited Hart who came from Kentucky. But it didn't suit French-Canadian Tommy Burns who took six months to get Hart into the ring at Los

Right **James J. Jeffries (World Champion 1899-1904).**

Angeles in 1906. Over 20 rounds it was Burns, whose career record looked far busier and more substantial than Hart's, who won a good points victory.

Burns went off, taking his title on a world tour. That was preferable to the awesome Jack Johnson catching up with him before he was able to make some cash from the title.

After his mauling by Jack Johnson in Sydney, Burns, and who can blame him, took a year and a half off. Then he had a fight a year until he was knocked out by Joe Beckett in London in 1920. Burns had had his first professional bout in 1900, and even at 39 was ready to back his chances of beating Beckett.

The stocky Burns liked to think he looked like Napoleon. I think it may have been just as well for Burns that Johnson didn't get to hear of that otherwise he'd have had nowhere to put his right hand.

Right **James J. Jeffries (right) outpoints Tom Sharkey over 25 rounds in his first defence of the world heavyweight title.**

But while Johnson was cavorting round Europe, the hunt was on, back in the United States, for the great White Hope who would put Johnson where he belonged. And as painfully as possible.

Eventually they found him, and it was rather ironical that the man concerned turned out to be one of the poorest of all the heavyweight champions, and yet he was to topple one of the best.

The name, of course, of immortal memory, was Jess Willard. When not much more than a lad, Willard decided that he was going to become world champion. At least that's how the story goes. So he went along to a manager, and asked to be put through his paces. What he went through were the ropes, all 6ft. 6in. and 17st. (238 pounds) of him. Half a round was enough for Willard.

But he had courage. He came back. He was big, but he was slow. He also had the good luck to catch Johnson, whatever the truth of the Johnson stories about throwing the fight, when Johnson either didn't want to know or was well past it. To the astonishment of everybody the cowboy from Pottawatomie County, Kansas was in the bigtime.

Willard won the championship in April 1915, but for all sorts of obscure reasons he defended it only once in the four years before Dempsey restored some degree of dignity to the whole business. That one defence was against Frank Moran, the character who got nothing when he fought Johnson in Paris. Willard's handlers weren't exactly letting him stick his neck out with that fight, either. Willard kept the title on a no-decision ten-rounder. The only way Moran could become champion was by knocking Willard out. Big deal.

But the real big deal came when Willard tangled with Dempsey. It was worth 100,000 dollars to Willard!

Far left **Tommy Burns (World Champion 1906-1908).**

Left **Jess Willard (World Champion 1915-1919).**

From Dempsey to Louis

JACK DEMPSEY lost his title in September 1926. Joe Louis won it in June 1937. In those 11 years there were six world champions, heavyweights who won the biggest individual prize in sport.

There was Gene Tunney, the cool, calculating United States marine. There was Max Schmeling, the only German to have ever been world champion. He was followed by Jack Sharkey, the only scrapper to be disqualified in a world heavyweight championship ring. Next was Primo Carnera, the Italian freak. Then there was Max Baer, the playboy from Nebraska. And finally James J. Braddock who suffered in the knowledge that he was only champion until such time as he was forced to get into the same ring as Joe Louis.

It wasn't a vintage period for only Gene Tunney had any pretensions to be compared with the world's greatest. I've always said that you can't get anywhere in boxing unless you're in love with the game. Well, if there are exceptions to every rule, then Tunney is the exception.

Tunney had one bit of luck. He was born with a good brain. He grew up on the sidewalks of New York before the first world war. Like everybody else he wanted to get out of it. He saw boxing as the way to do it, and succeeded. Then once boxing had served its purpose, and had set him up financially, he retired, world champion notwithstanding.

He even refused the offer of more than a million dollars to make a comeback. Later, after marrying a wealthy heiress, he became president of several wealthy companies.

He won everything except popularity. His failure to achieve that was because of the same old circumstances. They happen time and time again in boxing. He was never forgiven for beating hero Jack Dempsey.

Not that that would ever bother Tunney. He'd calculatingly waited until Dempsey had been softened by his life-style. Then, and only then, did he accept promoter Tex Rickard's bait for the fight.

Tunney had lost only one fight in a career that had begun in 1915. That was when he surrendered his American light-heavyweight title to Harry Greb. But it was only temporary. He regained it, and then outpointed Greb again to emphasise his superiority.

Like his arch-rival Dempsey, the young Tunney had stared poverty in the face. His parents had arrived in the United States from County Mayo. They settled in New York's Greenwich Village, and the young

Left **Giant Italian heavyweight Primo Carnera rocks Reggie Meen with a left in this bout at the Albert Hall, London on 18 December 1930. Meen was knocked out in the second round.**

Right **Gene Tunney (World Champion 1926-1928).**

Below **Gene Tunney defeating Harry Greb in December 1923. Greb decisively won the light-heavyweight title from Tunney in their first meeting, breaking Tunney's nose in the process, but Tunney won the return bout and three more to prove his superiority.**

Irishman went off in the war to become boxing champion of the U.S. Marines.

When he came back, he won all his early fights. The future should have been golden. It didn't seem so then, for Tunney lacked crowd appeal. But he took time off from reading, Shakespeare among other authors, to reflect that a personality cult was not a must as long as he kept winning.

He bought books on boxing by Corbett, Jeffries and Fitzsimmons. He studied anatomy, then in its infancy as far as applying it to boxing was concerned. He studied dieting which nobody had ever done before.

There was no smoking. No drinking. Girls were out. He kept fighting, and he kept winning. In 1924 they brought Georges Carpentier across, and Tunney knocked him out in the 15th round.

The record books give another clue to Tunney's single-mindedness. He had no less than five managers, and that's a statistic that proves who the boss was.

Tunney bought up films of Dempsey's fights and spent hours watching them. He worked it out that the punch to take Dempsey with was the straight right hand so he spent years working on it. It became the first punch he hit Dempsey with, and the 'Mauler' has since admitted that it almost finished their first fight in the first round.

Above Gene Tunney
leaves the ring as his
challenger, Tom
Heeney, is revived
from the 11th-round
knock-out.

Left Gene Tunney
returns to be declared
the winner. This bout
on 26 July 1928 was
Tunney's last before
his retirement as un-
defeated champion.

Right **Max Schmeling (World Champion 1930-1931).**

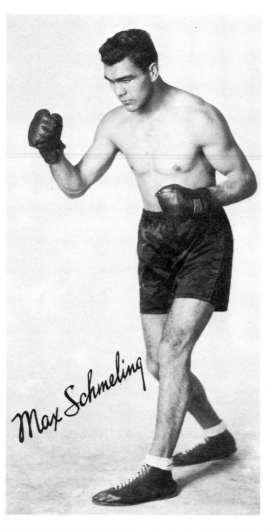

Max Schmeling

Below **Jack Sharkey (left) is disqualified for a foul on Max Schmeling in their championship fight on 12 June 1930.**

The far from genial Gene hadn't missed a single trick. He even hired some of Dempsey's sparring partners! When the fight was over and all the initial excitement had started to die down, the side of Tunney's character that he kept from public view influenced him to make arrangements to visit the beaten Dempsey's hotel the following morning to offer condolences. And threatened not to go through with the visit if it became a news story for the papers.

As one pro to another, Dempsey was grateful. Two weeks later, both Tunney and Dempsey were in the ring at Madison Square Garden to receive belts commemorating their title successes. Dempsey, so popular now, was cheered. Tunney was booed.

Tunney vowed then that if boxing fans wanted to boo him then they should pay for their pleasure. He decided, and bent the rule only very occasionally, that he would never go into a boxing ring unless he was on half the gate receipts. Tunney should be every boxer's example of how to finish. His son John rose to be a congressman in the United States senate. But that was all in the future.

Next was the not inconsiderable matter of the return with Dempsey in September 1927 after which Tunney gave promoter Rickard his cheque for 9,554 dollars and 46

Above and left **Two views of Max Schmeling's defence of his title against Young Stribling on 3 July 1931. Schmeling (right in both pictures) retained the title when the referee stopped the fight in the 15th round.**

Right **On 28 June 1932 Jack Sharkey (left) avenged his earlier defeat by Max Schmeling by taking the world heavyweight title on a split points decision.**

Below and above opposite **Four months after losing the championship Schmeling powered to an eight-round win over American heavyweight Mickey Walker.**

Below opposite **Schmeling (right) beats Walter Neusel in eight rounds on 26 August 1934. His supporters claimed he was consequently the logical opponent for the champion, Max Baer, but no match took place.**

cents. That was so that Rickard could add it to Tunney's purse of 990,445 dollars and 54 cents and write Tunney a cheque for one million dollars.

Naturally, Tunney had his own explanation for what was going on during the period of the famous long count. He is reported as saying: 'I only stayed down because Jack was tired and needed the rest'.

Promoter Rickard organised a series of eliminating bouts, and made a dollar or two on the way no doubt, to find Tunney's next title challenger. The dubious and painful honour was won by New Zealander Tom Heeney. Tunney proved himself the best boxing champion since the days of James J. Corbett by taking the unfortunate Heeney apart. Just before the end of the 11th round, the referee stopped the cruel slaughter.

26 July 1928 was an historic date. It was the last time Gene Tunney was seen in a ring. One of the punches in that fight rattled his brains and immediately he decided that enough was fair enough. Tunney certainly wasn't going to take any chances with his health.

In later years, he suffered from deafness. But so do hundreds of thousands of non-boxers!

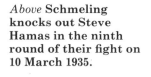

Above **Schmeling knocks out Steve Hamas in the ninth round of their fight on 10 March 1935.**

That left the cupboard extremely bare. There was money to be made, but where were the boxers to make it? Tunney and Heeney had been a financial flop for Rickard, so he started eliminations that were to leave the world without a champion for almost two years after Tunney's last fight.

Tunney's successor was Max Schmeling who was declared champion sprawled on his bottom. The new champion's first movement as theoretically the most dangerous man in the world was towards his corner in the arms of his seconds, for referee Jim Crowley had disqualified Sharkey for a low blow into Schmeling's stomach in their title fight in New York in 1930.

Schmeling kept the title a couple of years before being outpointed by Sharkey of all people in 1932. Perhaps he wasn't a great champion, but he's always argued that he deserved a term as title-holder if only for the manoeuvring that kept him away from Louis for longer than necessary.

Schmeling waited a long time for it, but he had the last laugh on the Americans. He did so well in business in Germany after the

Right **Schmeling sends a left jab to the face of Uzcudun in their bout on 7 July 1935 which Schmeling won on points.**

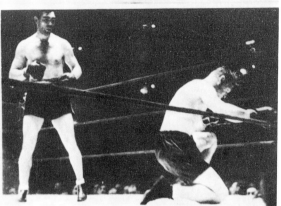

Left **The sequence shows the knock-out in the eighth round of Harry Thomas by Max Schmeling in New York on 21 December 1937. Within six months both boxers had unsuccessfully fought Joe Louis for the championship.**

war that by the 1970s every bottle of coke exported from the States to Germany had to go through Max's company.

Schmeling started fighting in Germany in 1924, but though he was German champion within four years he most likely wouldn't have been regarded as anything exceptional but for that 12th round knock-out of Joe Louis in 1936.

The more you look back on it now the more astonishing it gets. By the record book Schmeling had passed his peak, and although Joe hadn't yet won the world title he was knocking down everything in sight. He had all the physical advantages and was nearly nine years younger.

Yet Schmeling had studied boxing. He knew what it was about and he'd worked it out that Louis was open to a right-hander. He shocked Louis with one in the early rounds of the fight, and Louis never recovered.

Louis might also have wondered what manner of man he was fighting because while Schmeling was waiting in his dressing-room to be called out for the fight his trainer dropped dead from a heart attack. It had no outward effect on Schmeling. By that time his Teutonic brain was tuned in to a course of action that meant victory. The needle was already playing the music and the man from the master race was already programmed in.

Left **Jack Sharkey (World Champion 1932-1933).**

121

Right In 1926 Jack Sharkey beat the leading black heavyweight Harry Wills to earn a fight with ex-champion Jack Dempsey.

Below Jack Sharkey (left) looks on as British challenger Phil Scott claims he has been fouled in their title eliminator in February 1930. Referee Lou Magnolia awarded the fight to Sharkey.

Left **Primo Carnera (left) is declared the new heavyweight champion after knocking Sharkey out in the sixth.**

Below **Primo Carnera (World Champion 1933-1934).**

That was Schmeling's peak. Six years earlier he'd been behind when Sharkey was disqualified in the fourth. Max had given a better impression when defending his crown against Young Stribling in June 1931 at Cleveland. Max was trailing after five rounds then remembered he was supposed to be the world champion and gradually battered Stribling to the canvas with only seconds of the last round left.

Twelve more months go by, and then, leaping back onto the merry-go-round is our old friend Jack Sharkey who takes Max's title with a none too unanimous points verdict. That's the last time Schmeling appears in a world championship bout apart from those brief, dramatic 124 seconds with Louis in June 1938.

Jack Sharkey, born Joseph Paul Zukauskas in New York State two years after the turn of the century, never, I'm given to understand, took umbrage at being described as one of the most undistinguished of world champions. Which is just as well. For I gather he had a short fuse, temperamentally, and that was what stopped him being the boxer he could have been.

The first time the great big world outside the United States had to sit up and take notice of Sharkey was when he beat Harry Wills, the big Negro Jack Dempsey's stable were not keen on meeting. That opened the way for Sharkey to get himself a crack at Dempsey in 1927 when Dempsey was shifting aside rivals for another tussle with Gene Tunney.

Sharkey was lucky to get caught up by the Dempsey bandwagon because the fight

Right **Primo Carnera knocks out Boston heavyweight Ernie Schaaf in the 13th round. Schaaf later died of his injuries.**

became the first non-title event to gross more than a million dollars. The Yankee Stadium was packed with 75,000 fight fans and with all respect to Sharkey, it wasn't really him they'd come to see.

Sharkey started well. He was fast, and bright enough to keep out of Dempsey's way. Then came his mistake. He decided to take on the old champ. He moved in closer, close enough for Dempsey to start tattooing Sharkey's stomach with red blotches. Sharkey wasn't keen, remember, and he turned his head to protest to the referee that he'd been fouled. Turn your back on Dempsey...! Sharkey never saw the knock-out punch coming.

That action of Sharkey's takes on a new significance when measured against his title eliminator against England's Phil Scott at Miami in February 1930 when the vacant title was up for grabs.

Sharkey was due to meet Schmeling, but it was decided that Scott should have his chance and after he and Sharkey had been at it three minutes the decision appeared the right one. Sharkey was being outboxed.

Came the second round and it is obvious that Jack wasn't happy with the way things were going for him. He dropped Scott with a punch and what some suspicious folk might call a shove. In the third round a left hook crashed into Scott, roughly in the area called the lower stomach. Scott called for a foul. Instead of satisfaction, what he did get were two more belters in the same region.

Scott refused to climb back on his feet,

protesting that both blows were fouls, too. The referee, with the unlikely boxing name of Lou Magnolia, asked Scott whether he wanted to go on or not.

Scott said he did but, when yet another punch tore into his mid-section, he stayed on the canvas while the referee gave the fight to Sharkey, officially on a knock-out.

So Sharkey got his title fight with Schmeling who was to know just how Phil Scott, 'Phaintin' Phil' as the Yanks dubbed him, felt after a collision with Sharkey's fists.

Sharkey had gone off, drawn with Micky Walker and beaten Primo Carnera, and was considered to have done enough to be worth putting in with Schmeling again. The end of that confrontation, at Long Island in June 1932, was, astonishingly by Sharkey standards, not until the end of 15 full rounds. Perhaps not too full. It is reckoned to be one of the dullest title fights of all time and the statistician who counted the punches that were landed didn't need a calculator. There were 32 ... and for those who haven't got a calculator that is two punches each three-minute round.

Sharkey still hadn't finished surprising the punters. His next fight, in June 1933, cost him his world title. He fought Primo Carnera whom he'd outpointed nearly two years earlier. The record books have it that Carnera ended the entertainment with a right uppercut in the sixth round. Now Carnera was 6ft. 5¾in. Sharkey was six inches shorter. So where Sharkey's face

Left and below left
**Despite his great
advantage in height
and reach Carnera
could only defeat
Tommy Loughran on
points in his second
title defence on
1 March 1934.**

was when Carnera started that uppercut . . . the mind boggles!

Primo Carnera, the Ambling Alp from the Italian village of Sequals, is the guy everybody has to feel sorry for. He never pretended to be what he wasn't, but was a circus freak, a performer, a strong man, a wrestler. Carnera wasn't the tallest heavyweight champion of all because Jess Willard was a quarter of an inch nearer the sky. But, usually weighing-in at just over 19st. (266 pounds), Carnera was certainly the biggest.

Yet with all that bulk, Carnera had a problem. He just couldn't take a punch. Because of that they accused his handlers of fixing some of his fights, but there surely wasn't any way Sharkey or any of the other fighters of the time were going to chuck away the world crown. Even in the early 1930s, when it was not long after the Wall

Street financial crash, the title was worth a million dollars and more.

Carnera was launched in Paris in 1928. He'd been discovered in a French circus, where he was wrestling, by a Frenchman who was a former professional boxer. By 1929 he'd been introduced to London, and by January 1930 he was having his first fights in the United States.

If the crowds found it difficult to take poor Primo seriously, then his American handlers didn't.

Record books don't lie all that often and 'The Ring', the boxing bible, accounts for no less than 26 so-called contests in 1930. In March, for instance, he performed six times. The first was a sixth round knock out. The other five were all finished by first or second round knock-outs. Carnera certainly gave the customers value for money by knock-outs!

In 1932, Carnera was again on show 26 times. I don't know why they didn't break the record, because he fought on 29 December and again on 30 December. What they were doing on 31 December, I don't know, unless they were too busy counting the cash to worry about records.

Yet six months later, in June 1933, Carnera was winning the game's biggest honour from Sharkey.

Carnera's first appearance in Britain took the place by storm. It was October 1929 and he was put in with Jack Stanley, a local policeman from Greenwich. It was also top of the bill despite America's Frankie Genaro and Britain's Ernie Jarvis being there to fight for the world flyweight title.

Carnera sold the place out. Even the

Prince of Wales, the late Duke of Windsor, came along to see Carnera. Not bad for Jack Stanley. He was able to go through life boasting that he'd fought before the future king of England – even if it was for less than two minutes including the count. We think we don't miss many publicity tricks in these enlightened days. But we can still learn. The nicest Carnera touch of all was the use of pygmies to act as his seconds.

Nine months after winning the title, Carnera fought Tommy Loughran, the former light-heavyweight champion. Loughran wasn't supposed to be able to punch and was Lord knows how much lighter than the Alp. Yet he went the distance.

How the boxing public were expected to take this as serious boxing, I'll never be able

to appreciate. But what I am told is that Carnera's managers were on something like 95 per cent of all earnings. Except once. Carnera took the title back to Italy to defend it in Rome against Paolino Uzcudun, the Basque. Dictator Mussolini 'requested' that Carnera donate his purse to Fascist youth organisations.

But the nice side of the Carnera saga is that he eventually made a packet of dollars. The arrival of television and Carnera wrestling on coast-to-coast hook-ups made the likeable Italian a fortune to compensate for all the cash he made for others over there in the 1930s.

Those others include, of course, the promoters of the title fiasco between Carnera and Max Baer at Madison Square Garden in June 1934.

Officially Baer won the title by a knockout in the 11th round. At one stage before that, both boxers were on the floor of the ring. One had been punched there. The other had arrived with the assistance of a missed punch which had cost him his balance. At that stage, so the story goes, Baer the clown said to Carnera: 'Last man up's a cissy'.

Baer, who could never take anything seriously, always insisted, with a straight face, that he had found Carnera's weakness in 1934 when they were acting together in Hollywood. The film, and I'm not kidding, was called: 'The Prize Fighter and the Lady' (retitled 'Every Woman's Man' in Britain). Baer was the star, prophetically, and Carnera was the stooge (Myrna Loy played Baer's wife and Jack Dempsey also appeared). Carnera hit the canvas 11 times before conceding his title to boxing's best known playboy.

But Baer had enough sense to hang on to the crown for 12 months before defending it, and losing it to James J. Braddock who brought some of the old lustre back to the business of being heavyweight champion of the world. Later, Baer went on to fight for several more years until retiring to enlist in the United States army.

Baer, who was of German-Scottish descent, faced Braddock, an Irish-American who revealed late in his life that he was actually born in Britain's Manchester, in a clash at Madison Square Garden in June 1935. Twelve months earlier, when Baer was going through his comic routine with Carnera, Braddock, who had fought unsuccessfully for the light-heavyweight top spot six years earlier, was virtually thinking himself into retirement.

But then he was asked to change his mind, and a couple of good fights put him into the ring with Baer in 1935. On merit, Schmeling should have been there instead of Braddock but the anti-Nazi feeling was growing. Louis, naturally, had the best

Right **Max Baer (left) attacking James J. Braddock in his first championship defence. Baer lost his title on points.**

claim of all, but there was the suspicion that the time was not yet ready for the first negro champion since Jack Johnson.

So the scene was set for the Cinderella Man, one of the most likeable of guys. He had to believe in miracles for in the year before taking the Baer fight he was on poor relief and having his milk bills paid by his ex-manager.

Baer, his mind on higher things, thought the fight was going to be easy. He didn't bother to train. Braddock's wife didn't even bother to listen to the fight on the radio . . . so little faith. But when she turned the set on again an hour later, she was just in time to catch her husband's moment of triumph. Braddock had done it on points to become the fifth different heavyweight champion of the world in five years.

It was going to be so different when Louis laid his inevitable hands on the championship. Braddock had that feeling, too. He did his deal for a percentage of the Brown Bomber's future earnings. That was yet another delay for Schmeling's last title fight.

Braddock duly turned up in Chicago on 22 June 1937, a date of destiny for boxing. He lasted, bravely, for seven rounds, plus another minute and ten seconds. Then, he was unconscious on the canvas, put there by a bone-crunching right. Joe Louis had begun his reign.

Left **James J. Braddock (World Champion 1935-1937).**

Left **Braddock's only bout after his defeat by Louis was against Tommy Farr, who had recently survived 15 rounds with Louis. Braddock won on points over ten rounds.**

Charles and Walcott

Ezzard Charles, from Lawrenceville, Georgia, and Jersey Joe Walcott, from Merchantville, New Jersey, have much in common. They were the world champions that separated Joe Louis and Rocky Marciano, they were both black, they were both underrated performers, and they both wore modesty like a cloak of goodwill.

But they are also unique in one particular respect. They were Joe Louis' own nominations to fight for the title he vacated when he retired originally in 1949. And Joe also had an interest in the promotion.

They met at Chicago in June 1949. Ezzard won nicely over 15 rounds, a points verdict that didn't seem to upset anybody. Neither Europe nor the New York Commission were too pleased with this, and though Charles beat three rivals, including one-time world cruiserweight champion Gus Lesnevich, he still lacked the universal recognition he craved.

Meanwhile, the tax man was after Joe, and that was why Charles found himself staring across the Yankee Stadium ring at the man who had put him up for the world title, the same world title that was now at stake, 15 months earlier.

He outpointed Joe Louis easily. Not only was it a night of nights for Charles, his manager Jake Mintz, one of the fastest talkers of all time, was so overcome with joy that he collapsed on the canvas unconscious. And Ray Arnell, a cornerman with an exceptional reputation, had been dreaming for years of the moment he'd guide a man to victory over Louis. He'd been unsuccessful with Max Baer, Jimmy Braddock and Jack Sharkey among others. But that was where the unlucky Charles killed his popularity goose. No way after that September night in 1950, was Charles ever going to be acclaimed. The magic was for other folk. Charles was the tradesman. A good, honest tradesman who perhaps was never much more than a blown-up light-heavyweight. Because of that, he wasn't easy for a slower, natural heavyweight to nail.

If you were boxing in the United States in the 1940s and 1950s, then Charles was the man you had to beat. If you hadn't beaten or couldn't beat Charles then you weren't going to make it. If you had licked Ezzard though, you were ready for the big one.

He kept going from 1940, when he was 19, to 1959, moving down the ratings, but in a dignified way, after fighting Jersey Joe twice more for the world crown and losing their last fight in 1951.

Charles had the blackest of black faces,

Left **Ezzard Charles (left) throws a left to the head of challenger Lee Oma. Charles won with a knock-out in the tenth round.**

131

Right **Ezzard Charles (World Champion 1949-1951).**

but from the middle of it shone one gold tooth. Rocky Marciano used to say that it gave him a target to aim at when Charles fought twice more for the title. Charles could argue that Rocky didn't hit it very often in the first fight in July 1954 when a lot of experts rated Charles at his peak. For though Charles lost the decision, Marciano took 56 stitches home to Brockton in his face.

When they met again three months later, it was a different Charles. Perhaps understandably, a lot of his aggression had gone and Rocky knocked him out in the eighth round. Incidentally, his great grandmother, who had been a negro slave, was still alive then.

Maybe Charles would have been a more positive world champion had not a boxer whom he knocked out in 1948 died without regaining consciousness. Charles, after that, was something of a loner, a great reader who liked his own company and, rare among boxers, a man who had sensitive fingers with a double bass.

Yet, when the glory boys have had their day, Charles can look back on 13 fights for world heavyweight titles. That can't be bad.

LOUIS		CHARLES
36	AGE	29
6 FT. 2 IN.	HEIGHT	6 FT.
	WEIGHT	
216 LBS.		182 LBS.
	NECK	
17 IN.		16 ½ IN.
	REACH	
76 IN.		74 IN.
	CHEST NORMAL	
42 IN.		39 IN.
	CHEST EXPANDED	
45 IN.		42 IN.
	FOREARM	
12 ¼		12
	FIST	
11 ¾ IN.		12 IN.
	WAIST	
37 IN.		33 IN.
	BICEPS	
15 ¼ IN.		15 ½ IN.
	THIGH	
22 ¾		20
	CALF	
14 ¼ IN.		13 IN.
	ANKLE	
10 IN.		8 ½ IN.

Left **Joe Louis and Ezzard Charles.**

Below **Charles (left) outpointed Louis to become undisputed champion.**

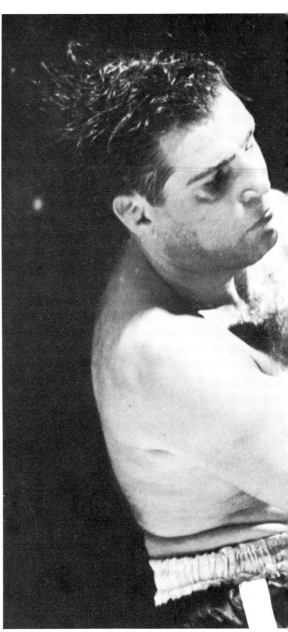

Above and below right
Charles' knock-out of Sam Baroudi caused Baroudi's death and left a lasting impression on Charles.

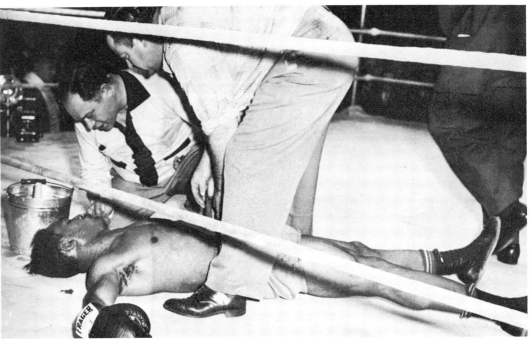

Left **Lee Oma (left) lost
his title challenge to
Ezzard Charles in 1951.**

Jersey Joe, on the other hand, stayed
around boxing to fight on for another couple
of years after becoming in 1951, at 37, the
oldest man to win the world crown. Old Joe
had made it at last, and he was a very
popular champ. But he lost the crown only
14 months later as the result of a com-
pulsory tangle with Rocky Marciano.

Walcott's title was only justice. Even Joe
Louis has conceded that he might have been
a lucky winner to get that very, very tight
verdict when Walcott challenged him back
in December 1947.

Walcott, father of six who later became
mayor of Camden, New Jersey, was a good
fighter to look at. The shape of a fighter I
think, starts with nice shoulders. Then the
body should taper down through a small
waist to thin legs. In other words, a triangle
from the shoulders.

That was how Jersey Joe looked, and it
took him many a time into the right
position to throw his famed left hook.
Properly delivered, that punch is un-
stoppable as Rocky Marciano found when
he successfully fought for Walcott's title.
Rocky had had 42 fights, most of them short
admittedly, but had never been on the
canvas in his life until Jersey Joe belted him
with a left hook in the first round.

Jersey Joe's success, socially as well as in
the ring, gave a lot of people a lot of pleasure. A deeply sincere man, Joe read the
bible in his dressing-room before his fights.
He had come up the hard way, really hard.
Born as Arnold Cream he gives his birth
date as 31 January 1914. But not even his
best friends believed him. And his boxing
records before 1930 have been conveniently
lost.

From 1930 until 1946, Walcott's fight
calendar throws up few names of any con-

Right **On 30 May 1951 Charles was knocked out by Jersey Joe Walcott who became the oldest man to win the title.**

sequence. He was busy learning and polishing. Then there was a points win over Joe Baksi in August 1945 – the same Baksi who was to come over to Britain and break heavyweight champion Bruce Woodcock's jaw – and Walcott was on his way.

He had a second go at Louis and got knocked-out in the 11th. There were two battles with Charles, both of which he lost on points before grabbing the ultimate prize when, surprisingly, the Pittsburgh audience saw him knock Ezzard out in the seventh round in July 1951.

The pay days were good, and Jersey Joe grabbed them. He outpointed Charles whose every move he must have known by then in their fourth fight. Having lost the title to Marciano, the old man had guts enough to accept a return in Chicago, but he was knocked out in the first round. That was enough. Jersey Joe had seen the light. He retired to devote himself to working for under-privileged children. At the same time he acted as a parole officer and, because of his integrity, was in demand as a boxing referee.

When I was growing up in South London and learning something about the fighting game, Walcott was one of the models that used to be cited to brother Jim and me.

Walcott, who swears that in his early days he was never knocked out by a punch but only by hunger, lasted so many years simply because he was such a talented professional. The sluggers, and I don't care who they are, even Rocky, have only got so many fights in them. Then they've got to quit, or be humiliated.

But if you're the right shape, you've got a few good moves, you can sling a left hook, then you can go on and on as long as you think it's worth it. Into that category I'd also put Archie Moore and Sugar Ray Robinson.

136

They're in a school of their own. They can go into a ring and they don't only fight, they box as well. They can look at the other fellow's punches and say: 'I don't want that one, I don't want that, I don't want that one', and they don't take them. They make the other blokes miss.

They don't take half the punishment that the average boxer does, and that's why they can go on for ever. Archie Moore, the former world cruiser champion who fought Marciano and Patterson for the supreme title, had arms like tree trunks. He hid behind and took punches on them. He was very rarely hurt, and the other geezer was out of breath long before the ageless Archie was.

Sugar Ray used to use his head – to miss punches. He bobbed. He weaved. He ducked. He was as difficult to nail as a wasp on the wing, and a darned sight more dangerous. In all ways he was a superb boxer.

From Rocky to Ali

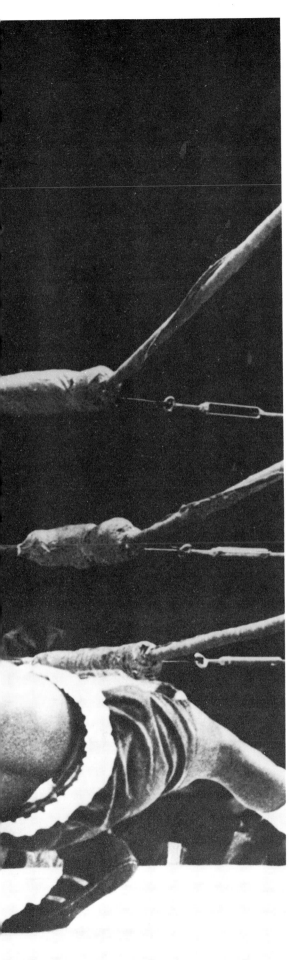

BETWEEN Rocky Marciano and the second coming of Muhammad Ali there were five world champions, Floyd Patterson, Ingemar Johansson, Sonny Liston, Joe Frazier and George Foreman. Joe Frazier, who was almost as good a musician as he was a fighter, was without any doubt the most underrated of them. And Sonny Liston, once the man everybody feared, eventually turned out to be the most overrated.

Putting Floyd Patterson on the same pedestal as Muhammad Ali would be impossible if they hadn't got that one factor in common – they are the only boxers who have ever regained the world heavyweight title.

Patterson was champion first between November 1956 when he knocked out Archie Moore in the fifth and June 1959 when Ingemar Johansson the Swede knocked him out in the third round. The title stayed in Sweden for just 12 months before Johansson went back to New York City and was knocked out in turn by Patterson, this time five rounds being enough.

There the similarity between Patterson and Ali ends, and Patterson has suffered from the comparison, especially when it has been Ali who has been doing the comparing! Yet I've got a lot of respect for Floyd. After all, James J. Corbett, Bob Fitzsimmons and James Jeffries all made attempts to regain their old title without succeeding; and those old-timers were a bit special.

Technically, Floyd is one of the best of the world heavyweight champions. And, now I'm going to surprise you, he has the fastest hands of any of them. Yes, faster even than Ali.

People who don't know boxing well get mixed up with this business of speed. Let me explain. Ali was fast, the fastest fighter on two feet, and that's the emphasis. Nobody quicker than Muhammad at getting round the ring. That's one kind of speed. But nobody quicker than Patterson at getting punches in. And that's another kind of speed.

Patterson's combination punches are a boxing legend. He had the speed to start with, of course. Manager Cus D'Amato just improved it.

And the way he did it was to give each of Patterson's punches a number. The right hook might be six. The left jab might be three. The uppercut might be five, and so on. Then Cus would start shouting. 'Three, five, one, eight', he'd go and Patterson would be packing the punches in. He's the only man I know who could put together a

Left **Joe Frazier's first championship defence was on 18 November 1970 against the world light-heavyweight champion Bob Foster. Frazier (standing) won in two rounds.**

139

cluster of eight or nine punches in two or three seconds . . . yes, as fast as that!

There isn't any way of developing this ability. It is born in you. It is a natural ability. But you can polish it.

Yet, mentally, Floyd whom I fought at Wembley in September 1966–he knocked me out with a beauty I never saw in the fourth round–was never fitted for boxing. He was too nice a guy. They say in boxing that Floyd was always ready to start apologising for knocking an opponent down. Though it's not quite true, certainly in my case, I can see what they mean.

The other story about Floyd which has been around boxing circles for years and has never been denied is this one: when he packed his boxing gear, and most of us do it in feet upwards order to make sure we don't forget anything, he'd finish with his dressing gown and would then put in a pair of dark glasses and a beard. Then, when he got to the arena, he'd seek out the promoter and ask for the back entrance so that if he

lost he could get out without anyone seeing him.

It's all wrong to go into a ring with a doubt in your mind that you might lose. Where's the disgrace in losing if you've given 100 per cent effort? If you're not mentally right, you don't often win. When you go into a ring, you've got to feel that you're going to win. If you've got many doubts, then maybe you shouldn't have taken the fight in the first place.

But, in spite of the fact that he won far more times than he lost, Floyd could never shake this feeling off. Yet, apart from that year of Johansson, Patterson was champion from 1956 until 1962 when Sonny Liston knocked him out in two minutes and six seconds of the first round.

Floyd never got over that, mentally again. I've heard it said too many times that Floyd was a lucky champion, and his success is just put down to shrewd Cus D'Amato's match-making ability which I'm the first to admit was rather tasty. But in his own right,

Patterson was a good mover. We know he could put his punches together well. He had a good left hook, and I know his right carried a knock-out drop in it. But . . . that Liston!

Patterson just couldn't believe that any man on earth could knock him out in two minutes and six seconds, at least not without the aid of a sledgehammer. So, nine months later in July 1963, he fought Liston again.

This time, Patterson showed an improvement. Of four seconds! Liston ended it in two minutes and ten seconds! The mental scars never left Patterson, who was only 21 when he became world champion by knocking out veteran Archie Moore in five rounds to succeed to the title Rocky Marciano vacated.

Patterson made his first headlines in 1952 when he became Olympic middleweight champion at Helsinki. He made his last 20 years later when, for the second time, he was knocked out by Muhammad Ali. In those 20 years, Floyd's was an extraordinary career, judged by top standards. He was a pugilistic yo-yo.

When he cracked Moore down in 1956 to become champion, Patterson had a string of 31 fights behind him, the only blot on the book caused when the wily Joey Maxim outpointed him, a decision that was by no means unanimous.

After Patterson had given Tommy Hurricane Jackson, whom he'd beaten in a title eliminator, his chance for the crown and stopped him in ten rounds, came one of manager Cus D'Amato's more inspiring pieces of match-making manipulation.

Pete Rademacher, who had won the gold medal at the 1956 Olympics in Melbourne, turned professional – and made his debut fighting Patterson for the world title. Patterson, of course, was never in danger. He knocked out Rademacher in the sixth.

Still, the money would be some consolation for lucky Rademacher, wouldn't it? Except that poor Pete didn't get any. It

could only happen in boxing I suppose, but when they worked the finances out, there was nothing left for the Olympic champion.

Patterson was on a quarter of a million dollars guarantee. And got it. The net gate was 210,000 dollars. So there was a 40,000 dollars loss for the promoters, and nothing for Pete.

I've heard plenty of boxers say they'd fight for nothing for a chance at the world title. But, as far as I know, Rademacher is the only one who has.

There were another couple of comfortable title defences for Floyd, against Roy Harris and Britain's Brian London, and then came one of D'Amato's miscalculations. In 1959 he allowed his man into the ring with Ingemar Johansson, then the European champion with a thumping right-hand punch we used to call 'Ingo's Bingo'.

Johansson had knocked out championship contender Eddie Machen in the first round of their contest nine months earlier, but nobody expected Patterson to be in

142

much danger. Though looking back the fact that first Rademacher and then the unsung Harris had both been able to floor the champion should have suggested that his chin wasn't punch-proof. For two rounds against Johansson nothing much happened. Then, in the third, Ingo got his Bingo through Floyd's defence.

Patterson went up and down again six times before the referee moved in and stopped the fight, and although Johansson was to lose the title after a year, he had equalled Jack Dempsey's record of seven knock downs in the same round of a world heavyweight fight. Luis Firpo was the victim, remember.

The Johansson fight went on at the Yankee Stadium, New York and has its own special place in boxing history. It was the first time that more money, in this case much more money, was made from television than through the stadium box-office. New-style big boxing was born.

With the audience potential of Europe

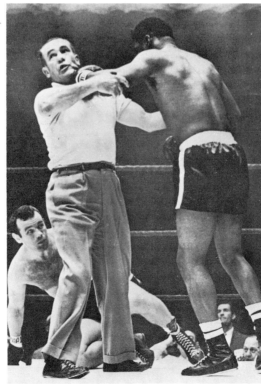

The third match between Patterson and Johansson saw both men in trouble. *Above* Johansson (left) drops the American for the second time. *Left* The Swede is felled in his turn (see overleaf).

143

Above **Johansson hits the canvas in the sixth (see preceding page).**

Right **Patterson put challenger Tom McNeeley (left) down ten times in the four rounds the 'contest' lasted.**

Above opposite **Sonny Liston (left) pounds Nino Valdes to defeat in August 1959. It was Liston's 18th successive win.**

Below opposite **Muhammad Ali (then Cassius Clay) hits Liston with a left in their first fight.**

beckoning, there could be only one sequel – a re-match. Because of the television circumstances, and a contractual agreement imposed by the sharp D'Amato, Johansson had to go back to the States to defend the title.

Mind you, Johansson was a bright lad, too. If the issue was home advantage or more money . . . well, Ingo didn't become one of Sweden's most successful businessmen without some talent in that direction.

The second Patterson-Johansson maul was in New York again, but at the Polo Grounds. This time, Patterson had found another half-stone of weight, and this time he wasn't going to be taken by surprise.

Instead, Johansson was. Over-confident, he thought that what he'd done once he could do again. But in the fifth round, a set of Patterson combination punches stopped the big Swede in his tracks and finally toppled him.

This was in the summer of 1960 and, with the score at one apiece, it didn't need an Einstein to work out what was going to be boxing's next big money-maker. So the pair met for the third time, at Miami, in March 1961, having between them tied up the world crown for nearly three years. They both reckoned they needed more poundage, and both came in probably too heavy. It wasn't a good fight, and Patterson won when Johansson narrowly failed to beat the count in the sixth round.

Johansson was an interesting personality. On the surface he seemed a playboy. But in truth, that was all wrong. Sure he liked a good time, bright lights, plenty of adulation and all that. But he knew his talents and he knew their worth.

Like me, he fought in the 1952 Olympics at Helsinki. He achieved more notoriety than I did because he got disqualified for not trying when he met America's Ed Sanders and I made no showing. Ingo was also a good singer and actor, and could have made a successful career in either direction when he finished boxing had he not preferred to go into business.

It was in 1957 when I boxed him, for the European heavyweight championship in Sweden. I was to win that title later, but that was my first stab at it, and Ingo knocked me out in the fifth.

I lost that fight because of inexperience and Johansson's style. Johansson, you see, was a counter-puncher, not a good boxer to watch. He used to like all his opponents to make the fight. They had to go to him. They'd walk on to that right hand, and Ingo would look good.

If Ingo went forward slinging punches he looked terrible. If he had a guy in trouble, he used to find it very hard to finish it if he had to go forward. It seemed to me that Ingo's famed Bingo also needed the impetus

Left **Joe Frazier (World Champion 1970-1973).**

Above **Joe Frazier (left) easily disposes of Terry Daniels in four rounds.**

of the other fellow coming on to it for it to have its greatest effect. Strange, then, that Johansson got this reputation for being such a fearsome puncher when it revolved just round one punch that required assistance anyhow.

Ingo hadn't got a left. It was just a measuring string. It wasn't a jab. It wasn't a straight left. It was just a sort of flick. It wouldn't hurt you. You could get your little sister there and she would take it. But once he hit you with that right . . . bang.

That's what happened to me in Stockholm. We knew all about Johansson, so we'd done our tactics. I was going to wait, and he was going to come after me. So for four rounds I waited for him and he waited for me. Most of the time, there was an awful lot of air in between us.

And even when we were going through the motions in the fourth I can hear the hum of the crowd which can only mean they're talking and not watching the so-called fight. I get a bit worried about this. I can see us getting booed out of the ring. That's never happened to me, and I don't like the idea of it.

So, like a mug, I think somebody's got to make a fight of this, and it had better be me. So I do. But Ingo's crafty. It's an open air fight. The sun's going down. They've given me the corner facing it, and Ingo comes

Above **A typical Frazier stance as seen in his bout with Ron Stander (right). Frazier won by a knock-out in the fifth (see opposite).**

across – in more ways than one. The sun is just nicely in my eyes when he belts me one with that right hand. I didn't see it coming. I got up, but the referee stopped it.

That was where Ingo was at his best, and worst. The other side of the coin was revealed in one of the Patterson fights. He had Floyd in trouble. He went forward trying to finish it off, but he went forward like a novice, swinging great roundhouse punches. So, instead of hitting Patterson he was just clubbing him and couldn't make any real impact.

Though Johansson was a great puncher, and I don't think anybody can deny that, it had to come naturally. The basic way of

boxing, if you've got a punch like that, is to try and create the openings for it. Usually, you do this by going jab, jab, jab. But Ingo couldn't do this. So he had to wait until his opponent made his mistake and got within range of that right. Like I did, if you like.

Ingo was good for boxing when boxing needed characters. Patterson would do nothing between fights to get himself talked about. Sonny Liston, who was to come afterwards, was somebody very few people were allowed near.

But Johansson, with a love for life, was different. He broke all the rules. His glamorous girl friend Birgit, who later became Mrs Johansson, was in training

Ingo came back from the States, regained his European title by beating my old Welsh adversary Dick Richardson, and then called it a day in the middle of summer 1963 to go with Birgit to live in tax-haven Switzerland, count his money and make some more.

So, it was Patterson's title again. But, waiting in the wings while Patterson and Johansson made their odd dollar or two was Sonny Liston who won the title from Floyd in 1962 and lost it 18 months later to Cassius Clay when he failed to get off his stool and come out for the seventh round.

Liston, who lay dead in mysterious circumstances in his Las Vegas home for a week before being found by his wife early in January 1971, never had any pretensions to popularity. People didn't like him, and he didn't like people. It was as uncomplicated as that. He was one of those stony-faced, steely-eyed guys who could look at you and stare right through you. If looks could kill he'd stabbed you, poisoned you and shot you as well.

He was in the Jack Johnson class as a hated champion.

I suppose, really, it was all in the background. He was born in Arkansas, the son of a farmhand, and it's believed he was one of 25 children. He ran away to St Louis, and was in trouble with the law from then on.

It was when he was 18, and still inside Missouri penitentiary, that he was encouraged to take up boxing. At 6ft. 1½in. and getting on for 16st. (224 pounds) Liston was a force to be reckoned with and by 1953 he'd won the Golden Gloves. Then he turned professional.

This was what was waiting for Patterson when Liston got his chance at Chicago in September 1962 – a man with a grudge against everything and just about everybody. He was 25 pounds heavier than

Below **Ron Stander is hammered into defeat by Joe Frazier (right) in their bout on 25 May 1972 (see preceding page).**

camp with him. She even went to America with him. And if Ingo was in a night-club after midnight, and that wasn't all that unusual, she'd be there with him, too.

And the press photographers used to love him. Pictures of him and Birgit by the side of the swimming pool? Any time they liked.

By contrast, when did anybody ever see any pictures of Mrs Patterson? Or Mrs Cooper, for that matter. My wife Albina only saw me fight once. That was when I fought for the world title. It was an occasion, and because of that I asked her to be there. That was the only time. She knew she wasn't going to like it, and never came again.

Above **George Foreman (facing us) unleashes a furious attack on the champion, Joe Frazier. Frazier hit the canvas six times in the two rounds the fight lasted (see opposite).**

Patterson, and outreached him by more than 12 inches. Not even Cus D'Amato could keep Patterson away from Liston any longer. Patterson had superior skill and speed. Would they be enough?

We already know the answer to that one. Two minutes and six seconds. The Ugly Bear, to use Ali's favourite description, landed a few fast body punches and two explosive lefts, and Floyd was on his way down the ladder. Then came the second Liston-Patterson collision, and Floyd was even more rungs down.

By now, the press lads were firmly convinced that Liston was invincible. I can't say that I really blame them. Part of their job is to keep sport alive, and since Rocky's retirement boxing had been short of personalities. So, life being what it is, Liston was built up to a stage where he was larger than life.

Mind you, the record looked good, and nobody can take that away from Sonny. But within the game itself there was the feeling that somebody who could move around a bit could make Liston an also ran. But nobody voiced that opinion within baleful Sonny's hearing. Do you pull the trigger when the barrel is pointing at you?

The movers, the jabbers, the cuties as they call them in the United States, would have shown Sonny for what he was. But until Cassius, none of them would dare go into the same ring with him. Liston loved his opponents to go in and mix it. With that huge advantage in reach, Sonny could hardly lose out. He loved his opponents to go in and have a bundle with him. And he was so used to fighting in bars and places like that, that looking after himself without needing to use science was nothing but second nature.

According to the press, Liston had two heads and four sets of hands. Ali, however, beat Liston with his brains.

Clay started the Liston talk-in months before the fight, reduced the Liston camp-followers to utter confusion by his antics at the weigh-in, and on mental agility Liston was left in absolute perplexity.

And when Liston found Clay hurrying across the ring at the first bell, taking the action straight to him instead of warily backing off as most of Liston's other opponents had done, the Ugly Bear was stranded out there without the comfort of his honey pot.

In the third round, Clay caused a cut under Liston's left eye. In the fifth Clay claimed that he couldn't see too well because something had come off Liston's gloves into his eye. In the sixth, Clay had to be pushed into action by his second, Angelo Dundee, protesting that his vision was blurred, but it cleared and he started punishing Liston.

In the seventh . . . but there wasn't any seventh. Liston stayed on his stool and said his left shoulder was injured and his eyes were cut.

I reckon to be something of an authority on cuts around the area of the eyes. I hate being reminded of it. But I never knew a fighter who was much bothered by a cut below the eye. And I don't think there will be until blood starts to flow upwards and not downwards.

Americans and American boxing were quite happy with the result. Cassius might be the Louisville Lip and he might be getting on the nerves of a lot of folks, but nobody was sorry that Liston had been toppled. Nevertheless, even Liston was entitled to another chance and he got it at Lewiston, Maine in May 1965. It was his last big payday. After it, Liston was discredited as a box-office attraction.

Officially, Ali finished it in one minute and forty-two seconds of the first round. And not even Clay's taunts and threats could entice Liston off the floor.

Liston carried on with boxing. There was nothing much else he could do. He carried on winning, too. But there was never any chance that he was ever going to get near the top again. He had his last fight in June 1970, and was found dead seven months later. There was also heroin found in Liston's house. His was a sad story.

Boxing got more out of him than he got out of boxing.

It was in May 1965 when Ali larrupped Liston off the scene. Six months later there was the indomitable Floyd Patterson making yet another assault on the world title.

This was the fight in which Patterson was tortured unmercifully . . . when we saw the hateful side of Ali. He could have been much more kind, but he made Patterson suffer for 12 rounds before the referee, and the crowd, had had enough of the slaughter.

It was the last time that Patterson, who spanned the years between Marciano and Ali, was to fight for the title. Floyd has been maligned, but there have been a lot worse champions than he.

Patterson admired Joe Louis tremendously. He has always yearned for the same recognition from the white people that Joe has had. That is like standing in hell and asking for heaven. But Patterson has nothing for which to reproach himself. He gave boxing 100 per cent as he saw it, and carried on campaigning after the Ali fight.

As I've said, he came over to London and fought me. He stayed there with the top-liners through 1968, had a year off and then came back and boxed more lower-grade fighters.

What drove Patterson, of course, was the idea that while Ali was having his spot of trouble with the army people and the title situation was in a tangle, he might get another crack at his old crown. But he didn't.

Yet he did get another go at Ali, a non-title fight in 1972. By then Patterson was 37. Most of the hate had gone from Ali, although they never became the great friends Ali and Frazier have. Ali put Patterson out in the seventh round, and so Floyd left the ring for the last time.

Frazier, who won the Olympic heavyweight crown in Tokyo in 1964, never got half the credit to which he was entitled. Yet since Frazier retired, Ali, after those

three momentous battles with him, has never been short of praise for Frazier.

Joe was a better fighter than a lot of people believed. There wasn't a lot of finesse with him, but he was something akin to Marciano. Too many so-called experts, most of them outside the game, would always have it that Rocky was all punch, that he was not much more than a slugger.

Rocky had a lot of technique. There was more skill there than was generally appreciated, and so there was with Frazier as well. There are some pieces of evidence that can't be ignored and they all add up to this: anybody who could do to Ali what Frazier did has got to be some sort of fighter!

Remember this, as well. He fought Ali when Muhammad was at his best, and he even beat Ali with the title at stake. That, for instance, is something George Foreman couldn't do. The 'Thrilla in Manila' with Ali was one of the epics of all time – it just couldn't have been scripted. But Frazier's first clash with Ali wasn't all that far

Above **The new champion, George Foreman, walks away after beating Joe Frazier in two rounds (see preceding page).**

behind, and because of Frazier winning it, this must have been his most satisfying fight. When boxers fight the way Frazier fought and the way Marciano fought with the real instinctive style that adds up simply to all action, I think they've only got so many fights in them. The body will put up with so much, and no more.

I would be surprised if Joe disagrees with me when I say that he must have reached his absolute peak when he fought Ali in New York in 1971 when Muhammad, having climbed all the way back, was within one fight of regaining his cherished title.

When he went in with Ali then, Frazier had the ability and the prime physical condition to be able to take the best Ali could throw at him on the top of his head, yes his skull. So Joe took them there and won a unanimous verdict from the referee and two judges.

The immediate reaction from the ringside was that Ali could have nicked the verdict. But the ringsiders could only see Frazier's battered face. What they couldn't see was where Ali had his lumps and bumps which were all round his waist.

Frazier had paralysed Ali with body punching. Ali couldn't bear the pain. For hours and hours after the contest Ali lay on his bed with nothing but a light sheet over him. Anything else would have been too heavy. He couldn't wear trousers, he couldn't wear pyjamas even, when he finally got up.

The second Frazier–Ali clash was the non-title 12-rounder in New York in 1971 from which Ali got a points decision; and then came Manila.

There isn't much you can say about a man who has to be stopped from fighting when he can hardly see. The man's courage says it all for him. That was virtually the finish for Joe. He had one more fight, a big-money battle with George Foreman which had to be stopped in the fifth with Frazier in all sorts of trouble.

It was clear, then, that Frazier's heart was no longer in the game. Since he turned pro, Joe had been managed by Yank Durham, and when Yank had died something had gone out of Frazier. Durham, one of the best manager-trainers boxing has ever known, was a Svengali where Frazier was concerned.

It was Yank who saw the gold beyond the Olympic gold. He had plenty to work on. For a start, Frazier was a tough guy, and that's not a bad asset for any boxer. Then, as I've said, he had a hard head. And that's not bad, either.

Durham didn't have much to do about Frazier's style. It was unusual enough. He boxed out of a crouch. Allowing that most heavyweights are reasonably tall, Frazier's opponents were put at a disadvantage from the start, for Frazier, ducking and weaving in front of them with his head down, presented a much smaller target than usual. And while they were working out what to do about it, Frazier was knocking them cold. In his first 11 contests, he was taken beyond the third round only twice–and he won them all by knock-outs.

He had one special punch, too. Dare I say it again? It was the good old left hook, though I have Ali's word for it that that right hand could whip through a bit, too.

I've often been asked whether I think Joe's activities with his music group, night clubs, one-night stands, and all that, took anything out of him. I don't think so. Frazier the fighter was nobody's fool. There was too much at stake financially. And anyway, it was his way of relaxing.

Mine was driving big, powerful cars, and I never remember anybody complaining about that, though thinking about it now it was probably a darn sight more dangerous than what Joe was doing.

Once he was in the ring, Joe could put it behind him. He was a good fighting machine.

Smokin' Joe was different from most of us. Not many of us are the youngest of 13 children. Not many of us were married at 16. And nobody else can ever lay claim to being the first man to beat Muhammad Ali.

Joe became world champion when they finally cleared up the mess created by Ali's being stripped of the crown. He fought Ali's old sparring partner Jimmy Ellis in New York in February 1970, hitting him hard enough and often enough to prevent him being able to come out for the fifth round.

Frazier stayed at the top of the tree for three years until tangling with George Foreman in Kingston, Jamaica in January 1973. Up to then, the indestructible Joe had won 29 out of 29, all but four of them by knock-outs. That Foreman managed to club him out in one minute and 35 seconds of the second round adds up to one of the biggest fight upsets of all time, particularly as Frazier had been down six times before the referee stopped the contest.

How did it happen? Well, the way I see it, it is all a matter of techniques. Around that time you had four boxers, Foreman and Frazier, Ali trying to climb back to the top, and Ken Norton. Now when Norton, who

Below **George Foreman (World Champion 1973-1974).**

came from San Diego, California, ever went into the ring with Ali he always fancied his chances. Don't forget that he broke Ali's jaw when beating him on points in 1973. And when they met again six months later he took Ali the distance. He's Ali's bogeyman, if you like.

Against Foreman or Frazier, Norton might be belted out of sight, but Ali didn't scare him one bit.

It's just one of those things. Frazier probably worked it out against Foreman like this: 'He's got no finesse, but he's got a certain amount of punching ability. I can absorb punishment. With my head-down style I've been doing it all my life. So I can absorb his'.

The theory is good, but . . . Frazier had been idle for eight months and two easy title fights against Terry Daniels and Ron Stander might just have given Joe the idea that he was a shade further ahead of the pack than he really was. Foreman had started in the pro game straight from the Mexico Olympics where he'd succeeded Smokin' Joe as heavyweight golden boy, and had had five fights inside twelve months when he squared up to Frazier.

Behind him, Foreman had left a trail of destruction. Thirty-seven bouts had added up in the simplest way of all to thirty-seven victories and only two of them had lasted the full course.

Ahead of him, there was another trail of Foreman destruction, one that was to last less than five minutes.

That, briefly, with counts of embarrassing frequency, is how Frazier became exchampion of the world. At this stage, Foreman had got most of us confused. Just how good was he?

He was champion of the world. He was undefeated. He put his first challenger, Puerto Rican Jose Roman away in two minutes of the first round in Tokyo in 1973. Then he took on Ken Norton, the guy who gave Ali so much trouble, and all Caracas fight fans saw of Norton was one round and two minutes.

So when Foreman faced Ali at Kinshasa in October 1974 he'd fought less than five rounds in winning the title and retaining it twice.

But Foreman, knocked out in the eighth, lost his championship as Ali became only the second man to win the title back. Where did Foreman do it wrong? Or was he never as good as we thought he was?

I think now, in retrospect, that Foreman was never in love with the game. He liked the glory and he liked the finance, but

you've got to have more than that. You have to love the game in some strange way. Because that's what, when the going gets tough, gets you off the canvas and back at it. You've got to be able to get up off the deck and come back punching. But Foreman had never been down until Ali decked him. It must have been a bit of a shock, to say the least.

I think, also, that when Foreman did at last get round to the Ali fight, after waiting for that eye injury to heal, he could easily have been overtrained.

He'd been out in Kinshasha a long time. He ought to have gone into the fight in the peak of condition. Eight rounds should have been no bother at all. Yet, the most damaging exercise for any boxer is to be made to keep punching thin air. And Ali certainly made him do plenty of that.

Early in 1976, Foreman knocked out Ron Lyle in five rounds before repeating his victory over Frazier. But from then on he bothered less and less with the game, confirming my theory that once his big-money days were over, George was not too keen on the fight business.

Above **Joe Frazier (left) outpoints Joe Bugner in a non-title fight in London in 1973.**

153

Practically
Speaking

YOU DON'T make many enemies in the ring. There are fellows I've spent a lot of time fighting; we nearly always sorted things out sooner or later.

Right early on there was Joe Erskine, the Cardiff heavyweight. We even plagued each other in our amateur days. I had a lot of affection for Joe. I always said that if he could punch he could have been world champion.

As far as the British heavyweights were concerned, Joe was far and away the toughest of the lot. He gave me more trouble than all the Brian Londons, the Dick Richardsons and the Billy Walkers. Joe had a real poker face, and if you're a puncher that gets on your nerves a bit. Because you don't know how you're doing. You dug your best punches in, and you never had any encouragement from Joe whether you were hurting him or not. You could thump Joe with your Sunday punch, and there wouldn't be a flicker of emotion.

Joe would just shift and keep on the move. He'd go one way, and you'd think he was out of distance. Then all of a sudden he'd stick out a left and hit you.

There was one classic example of Joe's talent. They sent Willie Pastrano over from the States to fight Joe. Pastrano was really a light-heavy. He was the world champion at that weight, and the Americans all thought he was a super boxer. I was the first to spar with him in this country and, take it from me, he was good.

They asked me who I thought would win and I said: 'Erskine knows more about boxing in his little finger than Pastrano will ever know'. Pastrano got his boxing lesson. He didn't know which way Joe went. Unfortunately, Joe took one or two bad beatings later in his career. The beltings made him lose a little heart for the game.

Yet there isn't any way known to boxing that you can use to make a bloke a puncher. Punching is a natural thing, and it often follows that the faster the boxer is the weaker his punch might be. Some guys move so fast round a ring, the amateurs Dick McTaggart and Nicky Gargano for instance, that their feet are never in position to allow them to deliver a big punch. The leverage is never there.

Then it's all about the technique of punching. Joe, like so many more, had got brilliant timing. But it's not the timing that brings a punch, it's getting the weight solidly behind it. Punchers are born and not made. And it isn't anything much to do with muscles. You can get a little fellow like Jimmy Wilde, the Welshman who was

Left **Henry Cooper sends Joe Erskine through the ropes to retain the British heavyweight championship.**

155

Above **Joe Erskine (left) in trouble against Henry Cooper.**

Above opposite **Henry Cooper defeated Billy Walker (right) in 1967 to win his third Lonsdale belt.**

Below opposite **Henry Cooper and Jack Bodell (right) whom Cooper outpointed in 1970.**

world flyweight champion in 1916 and 1917. He was eight stone wringing wet. He had arms like matchsticks. Didn't matter. He was able to knock out welters never mind flyweights.

I suppose as far as the general public could see I had more rucks with Brian London, the Blackpool heavyweight, than any other British opponent I got involved with regularly. Yet towards the end we were sending each other telegrams with best wishes before fights.

The rivalry with Brian was another, like Joe's, that went back to amateur days. He was a big, strong, rough guy who had only one way of fighting and that was to come forward like a bull in a china shop, hoping to murder you, hoping to ride a steamroller all over you. Brian was a good winning fighter.

A good bully, if you like. It was never in Brian's disposition to be losing and then come from behind and win.

I'll guarantee that if you look up all his fights, those he's won he's won from the first round. You never saw him pull one out of the bag, or get up and hit somebody.

I always tried to make sure when I fought him that somewhere in the first round I

either hurt him or scared him . . . I'd hit him with one of my best punches. Or just miss him. If he felt the wind, then he went back in his shell. He was all apologetic and quite careful.

When he was younger he had more heart for the game. He lost a little of it, and when he went down in his fight with Clay I was most surprised, particularly when he was counted out. Unlike Joe, Brian showed it when you hurt him.

The other Welshman I used to get repeatedly mixed up with was Dick Richardson. He was European champion at one time. Dick was tall, around 6ft. 3in. and a tidy 15st. (210 pounds) most of the time. He was another of those dangerous characters. Not an awful lot of finesse, but extremely dangerous.

Old Dick always used to think he was back in the rugby scrum with his head. What a great nutter he was. I knew his thinking backwards. You could almost see it written across Dick's mind . . . if I can get one in in the first round, it'll have to be a very strong referee who would disqualify me. Particularly if it is a championship fight. And Dick was right.

If Dick cut the other bloke's eye, he got himself a mountainous advantage. He's done it to me, and when I was ready for it. Shrewd old Dick had to be on a winner. Imagine a championship fight. People have paid £20 a head for some of the seats. If the ref stopped it in the first round he'd more than likely have a riot on his hands!

But we all get on well. Let's face it, professional boxing is a rough, tough way of earning your living. You accept all these things, because to be quite honest I was no angel when I was in the ring. If I cut somebody I was going to trade on it.

Brian went on to own night clubs. Dick had a car business and was doing well. So am I, so we're all happy.

Johnny Prescott, the Birmingham lad, was perhaps a slightly better boxer than Richardson or London. But he got himself a playboy image and was never taken quite as seriously by the public as he should have been. He was a good looking guy when he first came into boxing. They tell me he was another great gambler. He had betting shops, but he's switched into the scrap metal business.

He was a game boy who could take a good punch. I caught him with several good left hooks to the body when I stopped him in ten rounds for the British title. Where a lot of guys would have gone down, he just grunted and groaned and hung on. He had two very

Right **Joe Bugner (right) outpointed Henry Cooper in their title fight on 16 March 1971. This was Cooper's last fight.**

Below **On 14 October 1958 Cooper caused an upset by out-pointing Zora Folley (left).**

good fights with Billy Walker, real ding-dongs.

Billy himself was never genuine championship material. He had just a crash, bang, wallop style. There was no polish or smoothness, but the one thing you always had to give him was that he gave the punters value for their money. He always went into the ring fit which made him a tough guy to fight. And he never stopped bustling forward all the time, bobbing and weaving from the hips and slinging punches. Although Billy never won a title, there weren't many times he didn't pack the hall. He was an East End boy and Londoners loved him.

The most awkward of them all, without any doubt, was Jack Bodell, from Swadlincote in Derbyshire. He took over the British championship when I relinquished it while I was having a temporary dispute with the Boxing Board of Control.

He was a southpaw, and I used to say that he won most of his fights not because he was a good performer but because he was just plain awkward. All southpaws are awkward. Some are more awkward than others and Jack was about the most awkward of them all.

Jack had a very wide leg stance, much wider than the usual heavyweight's stance. That meant that if you moved in to punch and he came forward it was quite likely that his foot would be behind you and he would trip you up. Jack also had this habit of stamping his foot as he came in. Being the southpaw that he was, he usually stamped on your toes! I used to have bruises as big as pennies on the feet and on the shins where his knees had hit me as he came forward.

Jack was not the most durable. I fought him twice and it was just a matter of biding time, picking punches, and waiting to get the left hook in.

With Joe Bugner, British boxing was unlucky. When you looked at him he seemed to have everything in his favour. He was a bigger man than Muhammad Ali. At 6ft. 4in. and 16st. (224 pounds) he was perfectly built. Yet to my mind he didn't have the heart. I don't think he really liked what he was doing. He came in a bit late at 17 years old, and I always had a sneaking feeling he would have been happier doing athletics. He was keen on that, particularly shot and discus events.

Joe had done a lot of weight training and was a bit too muscular on the top. He was too tight and too tense, and it was tragic for British boxing that once the

boxers of my era had retired he was unable to fill the gap.

He earned plenty, and for that he's got to thank Muhammad Ali for two fights. He got fortunes whereas if he'd been fighting ordinary fellows he wouldn't have got anywhere near as much.

Perhaps manager Andy Smith wasn't tough enough. Perhaps Joe needed someone like Angelo Dundee who could make Ali do what was right for him. Bugner, when he was in that ring, needed someone to call him everything, slap him around the face, stick a pin up his behind and tell him to get out there and do something.

Because I had such a long time at the top of the British scene, I fought more European and transatlantic boxers than most. They came in all shapes, from the roly-poly French champion Maurice Mols to the superbly-built Ali, but only one size – big.

I'd had nine fights and was still unbeaten when they brought Uber Bacilieri, the Italian champion, over to London in the spring of 1955. And I remember the fight for more than just the fact that Bacilieri wasn't a bad performer.

It was a landmark in my career because it was the first contest I ever lost because of

Below **South African Gawie de Klerk was knocked out by Henry Cooper in the fifth round.**

Above **Roy Harris (left) loses on points to Henry Cooper in 1960.**

Below **Argentinean Alex Miteff backs away from a blow by Cooper.**

a cut. Our heads clashed in the second round, and that was the end. Five months later Bacilieri was back in a London ring, and I'd seen enough in the first fight and the early rounds of the return to know how to play it. I knocked him out in the seventh.

Bacilieri hadn't got much of a punch. That didn't mean that I could take liberties, and I didn't. But he held his hands far higher than British boxers do. I needed only to get a good dig into his body and his guard was down.

He was an ideal opponent for me to meet at that stage of my career. The win, on paper, looked good, and with his style of fighting there wasn't much risk of my being in danger. Nor was I.

The next foreigner to come over, early in 1956 after I'd been outpointed by Joe Erskine in a British title eliminator, was Mols. He'd got nothing to lose, and I'd got everything to gain. He'd come in a shade overweight, and the old left hook finished it in the fourth.

But if Mols wasn't exactly memorable, then Italian Giannino Luise, with whom I had a brief encounter lasting less than seven rounds when the referee stopped the fight, was certainly less so. Like a lot of the Continentals, he had a big punch, but you could see it coming. And he weighed more than 15st. (210 pounds) which meant that he couldn't be the quickest of movers.

Then came Ingemar Johansson and my impatient encounter with Ingo's Bingo, that fearsome punch that knocked out so many of his opponents.

In the autumn of 1957, after four defeats in a row, I needed my confidence restoring. I wasn't exactly God's gift to British promoters at that time, so manager Jim Wicks and I embarked on three fights in Germany.

The first opponent was Hans Kalbfell. He was 6ft. 4in. and more than a stone heavier than I was. Although he was the German champion he was ponderous like most really big men and I produced some of the best boxing of my life to get a good points verdict. Heinz Neuhaus was next. He was a useful workman fighter, but I reckon I won nine rounds out of ten to get a home town draw! The third German was light-heavyweight Erich Schoeppner who was well on his way to defeat in the sixth round when I caught him behind the left ear as he was spinning off the ropes. They said the blow was illegal and disqualified me. Schoeppner seemed pretty useful. As the Germans withheld half my purse I never went back to take a second look at Schoeppner or any other German boxer.

It was time for my first tangle with American opposition. I was fixed up to fight the Argentinean Alex Miteff in London when he injured himself and could not make the date.

That was how I came to be inside the same ring as Zora Folley, who was ranked with Archie Moore as joint No. 1 contender for Floyd Patterson's world title. Maybe Folley and his handlers reckoned he was going to be on an easy pay day. But, if they did, they were wrong. I did him on points, and I

wasn't even British champion then.

That result couldn't have done anything for Folley's reputation back in the United States, but to a certain extent it was his own fault. For a couple of rounds he was doing well. His left jab had caught me several times, and I'd winced when he thundered in a right hand that sent me down for a good count.

I got up, which was where Folley, a fighter on the brink of a crack at the world title, made an astonishing mistake.

161

Above **A left from Cooper knocks out Chip Johnson in the first round of their bout in 1965.**

was a boxer and a fighter. He had a tidy left jab as he'd proved in the first couple of rounds against me. There was a knock-out in that left, and in his right as well for he had a cross that spelled instant sleep if you didn't see it coming.

When you consider that Folley could also stand up, box and take a punch, you had a guy who perhaps should have had a much earlier shot at the world crown. Many more less deserving ringmen have been luckier than Folley.

Perhaps his biggest handicap was that he never looked a good fighter. He got results, but he never put on the style. He never did more than what was just necessary to win. It was probably more a question of temperament, because his ability was there for everybody to accept without question. But when it came to the big one. . . .

Early in his career, Folley snatched verdicts over rated men, the trial horses like Nino Valdes, Wayne Bethea, Alex Miteff, Ernie Machen, Willi Besmanoff and Doug Jones. He reversed that defeat by me by coming back to London and knocking me out in the second round when I hadn't trained for the fight as well as I might. I

He forgot all about his left jab. He concentrated on trying to finish me with a huge right. It was a great tactical error. It gave me a chance to get the old left hand working and I got myself sorted out. More than that, I gave him a boxing lesson and got the nod after ten very good rounds.

I was pleased with myself after that one, for Folley was good. You don't get rated as highly as he was without being useful. He

Right **Hubert Hilton goes down in the second round of his match with Cooper.**

made the mistake, for the last time, of training at home.

But when he was just one step away from the title chance, the talented Folley lost out. Sonny Liston knocked him out in three rounds. Doug Jones came back and knocked him out in seven. Ernie Terrell outpointed him and Karl Mildenberger, of West Germany, held him to a draw.

Eventually, Folley got his chance. He fought Muhammad Ali for the world crown. But he was 35 years old then and over the hill.

He was 26 and in his prime when I out-pointed him, and I rate that as one of the best performances of my career.

In January 1959, I won the British and Empire titles at last by outpointing Brian London. I took a long break from the game because I was fighting for the tax man and then defended the Empire crown against Gawie de Klerk, who was a South African policeman.

He was a tough guy but not very well drilled in the finer arts of the game and when I began to catch up with him from the third round onwards I was confident about the outcome. The referee finally stopped the contest in the fifth round.

Roy Harris was champion of Texas when I fought him. He was more of a boxer than fighter and spent most of his time going backwards. Maybe I flatter myself, but it could be that somebody had warned him about my left hook. Eighteen months earlier he had been good enough to have fought Floyd Patterson for the world title, taking the champion to twelve rounds. He held a lot, too, and though he was un-doubtedly in the world's top ten for a couple of years he was one of the men who got a title fight for which Folley, for one, had better credentials.

I outpointed Harris and got the same verdict when I faced Alex Miteff just before Christmas 1960. Miteff was a right tough cookie. He'd been round the American circuit for ten years or so and knew all the tricks. The traditional Argentinean heavy-weight is not much more than a crude puncher who'll take six punches to land one which could easily be the knock-out. But not Miteff. He had a lot more going for him than just brute strength.

And talk! He was worse than Ali. I was younger, then. I'd never met anybody even

Left **Floyd Patterson (left) puts Cooper down in the fourth round of their fight on 20 September 1966.**

163

remotely like him. All through the fight, and I was being very careful not to lose my cool, he kept on . . .'Come on, son, let's have a fight'. When we got into a clinch, he was at it again . . .'Let's have a punch-up, shall we?'.

He was rugged, and if you were a youngster you'd fall for it. But I knew better, I kept that left going out, jab, jab, jab for nine rounds and was so far ahead there was only one way left he could win the fight.

So when I came out for the tenth I thought: 'Right, if you want a fight I'll come and join you'.

Then, bang. Straight on the jaw. Mine. Miteff had slung one and I'd bought it. In the corner, manager Jim Wicks was doing his nut. But I was all right. I gave my head a chance to clear. Got up. And jabbed out the fight. But it taught me a lesson. You go on learning all the time in this boxing game.

I suppose there was never a time when Miteff was seriously considered a title contender. But he was one of those awkward fighters that you had to meet and beat to prove you were worth a title shot yourself.

The next man the Americans sent over was Tony Hughes, a protégé of Rocky Marciano. But he didn't give me any

trouble and I stopped him in five rounds, the faithful left hook knocking him out.

A month later, early in 1962, Wayne Bethea, a big coloured fellow, crossed the Atlantic and he was a quite different sort of problem. Like Miteff, he was a thorough professional.

I got a points verdict from him, but I wasn't sorry he was past his best when I swapped punches with him. I could see why, in his younger days, he had fitted into that category of awkward fighters whom title contenders would rather not know about.

Characters like Bethea and Miteff are fine – if you beat them. But lose to them and not only have they made you look awkward yourself but they've probably put you back a year or two in the ratings.

They breed plenty of them in the United States but I had a rest from them in 1963 which was the year of Clay and the left hook that put him down.

I spent most of 1964 basking in the glory of being a triple champion, British, Empire and European, until they took the European crown off me because I wasn't fit enough to defend it against Mildenburger.

So I wasn't worried when they flew Roger

Rischer across the Atlantic to give me a paid work-out in the autumn. I lost it on points over ten rounds and I never want to be reminded of it. When I fought a stinker I confess I usually made a good job of it, but Rischer made life difficult.

He was a right spoiler. Not that he did much himself, except holding, hugging and cuffing, but he managed to stop me getting into anything like a smooth rhythm. It would have been easier fighting an octopus!

I was well into Americans at this time. Dick Wipperman came over early in 1965, I'll always remember him. Not because he was an exceptional fighter. He was a big cowboy who wore a stetson for publicity purposes.

Poor Dick, he was well over six feet tall and built like a tree. When I caught him with the left hook in the fifth round he straightened and I felt like shouting: 'Timber . . .!'

Nowadays, if I want to get a nice warm glow on, I think of Chip Johnson, a fast-talking American who had ended brother George's boxing career in Manchester a few months before I met him at Wolverhampton. He used the fight build-up to boast that what he'd done to one Cooper he was going to do to the other.

That was all right by me. You've got to have a bit of meanness, and to keep mouthing like that was the best thing he could do for me. It was the ideal incentive. At a press reception he was quite flash with it, giving the journalists all they wanted while I listened at the other end of the room.

It came to the fight, I hadn't even got a sweat on in the first round when he stuck the Johnson jaw out. It was right in the path of a left hook. That was one of the quickest knock-outs in my career.

Later in 1965 another Johnson, Amos, came over from the States. Like Rischer and subsequently Boston Jacobs, he was a spoiler. A couple of low blows didn't help either but although I was far from at my best, I thought I'd done enough to get the verdict. Unfortunately, the referee didn't agree with me.

Amos was followed in January 1966 by Hubert Hilton, an American ranked No. 9 in the world. I knocked him out with a left hook just over a minute into the second round.

Less than a month later, I was back in Wolverhampton taking on yet another American, Jefferson Davis, from Mobile in Alabama. He also had beaten brother George, so the revenge element was there again. He'd also lasted the distance with

title contender Ernie Terrell so there was no question of pushovers being lined up.

But Davis lasted less than two minutes of the first round, the victim of the fastest knock-out I ever achieved.

Wipperman, Chip Johnson, Hilton and Davis, none of them had ever been knocked out before. They'd lasted, respectively, five rounds, one round, two rounds and one round, so perhaps I'm not the best person to judge their capabilities!

After the cut eye had caused the world title fight with Ali to be stopped in the sixth, I met Patterson and that k.o. punch I never even felt.

In April 1967, I fought another rated American, Boston Jacobs, at Leicester. He was a strong boy. He came forward a lot, forcing it all the time. I got a points verdict over ten rounds but it wasn't one of my better fights. It was thought at the time that I might do better with a little extra weight so we allowed it to creep up to 13st. 12lb. (194 pounds), the heaviest weight at which I ever went into a ring. The experiment was a mistake. I was sluggish. But again I could understand why most of the leading boxers across the Atlantic didn't want to know about Jacobs. He was another

Above **Cooper is fouled by Piero Tomasoni in their championship battle in Rome in 1969. Cooper won by a knock-out in the fifth (see overleaf).**

of those you had to work like mad to beat yet look pretty ordinary while you were doing it.

The hints that I might eventually get a shot at Ali's world title had first been dropped in 1965 so I hadn't been too worried about the European heavyweight title they'd taken from me in 1964 when an elbow injury had prevented me from defending it.

But, by September 1968, I was more than ready to try and win it back from Mildenburger. He'd had a crack at Clay's world crown four months after I had. The line in form was that I'd lasted six rounds and the German had gone twelve before Clay had knocked him out.

I didn't think that was the difference between us. Mildenburger hadn't cut like I had and perhaps Ali had taken longer to fathom the southpaw style. I wasn't worried. I reckoned I could lay my hands on the title again, and I was right. Mildenburger was disqualified by an Italian referee in the eighth for butting.

I don't think it was intentional. The German was nearing the end of this particular road when it happened.

Mildenburger was probably the clasiest southpaw I've seen and certainly Germany's most significant contribution to world boxing since the days of Max Schmeling. He was smoother in style than most southpaws who usually look ugly because they're fighting the wrong way round.

He was big and strong and had a fair right jab. He was a durable performer, too. Ali had to wear him down and so, to a lesser extent, did I. He was also one of the best-looking boxers of recent times. He's made one or two films, and has also been used on television.

Mildenburger provided me with an unusual tactical exercise. Normally, when fighting southpaws, the theory is to change and use the right hand to lead with. But I decided to take him on with the left hand. It came off because I managed to get it in over his right. I was beating him to the

Below **Cooper knocks out Tomasoni.**

punch and, as the fight went on, Mildenburger's face began to puff up and an eye started to swell, all signs that my left jabs were finding their target. He began to get slightly ragged and was warned a couple of times before the top of his head opened a cut above my right eye, the cut which prompted the referee to award me the fight.

There were just two more fights against foreigners. The first was my one and only in Italy, my in-laws' country. It was against Piero Tomasoni for the European heavyweight title in Rome in 1969 and was the roughest, dirtiest brawl I ever got myself involved in.

Tomasoni was called the Axeman, and it was a fair enough nickname. He swung a right hand that started so early that you had time to duck twice.

But three times he hit me right in the middle of my foul cup, and that's roughly seven inches below my navel and the imaginary line below which you're not allowed to hit. When a foul cup leaves the manufacturer it is convex-shaped. When I took mine off after the Tomasoni onslaught it was concave! I knocked him out in the fifth.

Last of all, in November 1970, came the unique Spaniard José Urtain. It was again for the European heavyweight title which I'd resigned after the Tomasoni fight as cartilage trouble stopped me boxing.

In some respects Urtain, who came from the Basque country, was another Tomasoni, all right hand and very little else. He just slung the right hand and wasted a lot of energy. As he tired, the good old left hand was doing its job again and the referee stopped it in my favour at the end of the eighth.

But what made Urtain unique was that he was a rock-lifting champion. They go for rock-lifting in a big way, do the Basques. Urtain's father was also a champion rock-lifter. So was his grandfather. And one of his ancestors was apparently reputed to be the strongest man in the world.

It takes all sorts to make a world, especially the world of boxing.

Below **Cooper jabs Urtain to defeat to regain the European heavyweight title.**

Personally Speaking

IT SEEMS a long time back now to March 1971 when I fought the last one. It is I suppose. I haven't even got a boxing glove left in the house. They've all gone for souvenirs or charity.

But boxing has been very good to me. I don't think I'd change much. Boxing has taken me into Buckingham Palace and given me a nice six-bedroomed place of my own. I've been places and met people that I wouldn't have done if not for boxing.

It was tough getting to the top. I had to dedicate my life to it, and I don't suppose it is any easier now. If you don't cut out the dances and go easy on the drinks and the girl friends, you haven't much chance of succeeding in boxing.

My brother Jim and I probably missed a lot by being in bed at ten o'clock most evenings. But what you never have you never miss, they say. If you're really keen on something – it might be swimming or it might be athletics etc. – if what you are doing is giving you so much pleasure, then what are you missing?

When I turned professional all I wanted was a British title and then a Lonsdale belt outright. Then I became the only British fighter to win three outright, so all the years of hard work were worthwhile.

Do I resent the frequent intrusions into my private life? No. I don't mind the lime-light. Accept the fact that you're an entertainer.

To be a fighter, entertainer, you've got to be a bit of a show-off. And that's what I always was, I think. I've loved it. People wonder if it gets on my nerves other people constantly wanting autographs. I think the reverse. When people don't want to come up and speak to me, don't want to shake my hand, don't want to say hello, then I'm worried in case they've forgotten me. Every time you shake a hand or sign an autograph you make a friend.

Basically, you have to accept that you can never go out quietly. But the public are very good. They respect your privacy in a lot of ways. You know that when you go to a restaurant you're going to be recognised. Heads are going to turn. But most people will wait while you finish your meal before coming up and asking for autographs. That's marvellous!

I've also been very lucky in life by being blessed with an even temperament. I'm easy going. It takes a hell of a lot for me to be taken out of my stride. In a profession that lives on its nerves, I'm not so sure that hasn't been my greatest asset . . . and probably still is.

Left **In 1967 Henry Cooper became the only boxer to win a third Lonsdale belt. Here he is shown holding it with his manager, Jim Wicks, on the left.**

The Fighters' Records

Jack Johnson
(John Arthur Johnson)

Born 31 March 1878, Galveston, Texas

1899
11 Feb	Jim McCormick, d 7r, Galveston	
17 Mar	Jim McCormick, w disq r7, Galveston	
6 May	Klondike, l ko r5, Chicago	
16 Dec	Pat Smith, d 12r, Galveston	

1901
25 Feb	Joe Choynski, l ko r3, Galveston
7 Mar	John Lee, w pts 15r, Galveston
12 Apl	Charley Brooks, w ko r2, Galveston
6 May	Jim McCormick, w ko r2, Galveston
28 May	Jim McCormick, w ko r7, Galveston
12 June	Horace Miles, w ko r3, Galveston
20 June	George Lawler, w ko r10, Galveston
28 June	Klondike, d 20r, Galveston
	Willie McNeal, w ko r15, Galveston

1902
17 Jan	Frank Childs, d 6r, Chicago
7 Feb	Dan Murphy, w ko r10, Waterbury
22 Feb	Ed Johnson, w ko r4, Galveston
7 Mar	Joe Kennedy, w ko r4, Oakland
15 Mar	Joe Kennedy, w ko r4, San Francisco
6 Apl	Bob White, w pts 15r
1 May	Jim Scanlon, w ko r7
16 May	Jack Jeffries, w ko r5, Los Angeles
28 May	Klondike, w ko r13, Memphis
4 June	Billy Stift, d 10r, Denver
20 June	Hank Griffin, d 20r, Los Angeles
4 July	Hank Griffin, d 15r, Los Angeles
3 Sep	Pete Everett, w pts 20r, Victor, Colorado
17 Sep	Hank Griffin, d 20r, Los Angeles
21 Oct	Frank Childs, w pts 12r, Los Angeles
31 Oct	George Gardner, w pts 20r, San Francisco
5 Dec	Fred Russell, w disq r8, Los Angeles

1903
3 Feb	Denver Martin, w pts 20r, Los Angeles
27 Feb	Sam McVey, w pts 20r, Los Angeles
16 Apl	Sandy Ferguson, w pts 10r, Boston
11 May	Joe Butler, w ko r3, Philadelphia
31 July	Sandy Ferguson, no dec 6r, Philadelphia
27 Oct	Sam McVey, w pts 20r, Los Angeles
11 Dec	Sandy Ferguson, w pts 20r, Colma

1904
16 Feb	Black Bill, no dec 6r, Philadelphia
22 Apl	Sam McVey, w ko r20, San Francisco
2 June	Frank Childs, w pts 6r, Chicago
18 Oct	Denver Martin, w ko r2, Los Angeles

1905
28 Mar	Marvin Hart, l pts 20r, San Francisco
25 Apl	Jim Jeffords, w ko r4, Philadelphia
3 May	Black Bill, w ko r4, Philadelphia
9 May	Walter Johnson, w ko r3, Philadelphia
19 May	Joe Jeannette, no dec 6r, Philadelphia
26 June	Jack Monroe, no dec 6r, Philadelphia
13 July	Morris Harris, w ko r3, Philadelphia
13 July	Black Bill, no dec 6r, Philadelphia
18 July	Sandy Ferguson, w disq r7, Chelsea
24 July	Joe Grim, no dec 6r, Philadelphia
25 Nov	Joe Jeannette, l disq r2, Philadelphia
1 Dec	Young P. Jackson, w pts 12r, Baltimore
2 Dec	Joe Jeannette, no dec 6r, Philadelphia

1906
16 Jan	Joe Jeannette, no dec 3r, New York City
14 Mar	Joe Jeannette, w pts 15r, Baltimore
19 Apl	Black Bill, w ko r7, Wilkes Barre
26 Apl	Sam Langford, w pts 15r, Chelsea
18 June	Charlie Haughey, w ko r1, Gloucester
20 Sep	Joe Jeannette, no dec 6r, Philadelphia
8 Nov	Jim Jeffords, w pts 6r, Lancaster
26 Nov	Joe Jeannette, d 10r, Portland
9 Dec	Joe Jeannette, w ko r3, New York
	Billy Dunning, w pts 10r

1907
19 Feb	Peter Felix, w ko r1, Sydney
4 Mar	Jim J. Lang, w ko r9, Melbourne
17 July	Bob Fitzsimmons, w ko r2, Philadelphia
28 Aug	Kid Cutler, w ko r1, Philadelphia
2 Nov	Jim Flynn, w ko r11, San Francisco

1908
3 Jan	Joe Jeannette, d 3r, New York
11 June	Al McNamara, w pts 4r, Plymouth
31 July	Ben Taylor, w ko r8, Plymouth
26 Dec	Tommy Burns, w rsf r14, Sydney
	(World title)

1909
10 Mar	Victor McLaglen, no dec 6r, Vancouver
19 May	P. Jack O'Brien, no dec 6r, Philadelphia
30 June	Tony Ross, no dec 6r, Pittsburgh
9 Sep	Al Kaufman, no dec 10r, San Francisco
16 Oct	Stanley Ketchel, w ko r12, Colma
	(World title)

1910
4 July	James J. Jeffries, w ko r15, Reno
	(World title)

1912
4 July	Jim Flynn, w police stopped fight r9, Las Vegas
	(World title)

1913
19 Dec	Jim Johnson, d 20r, Paris
	(World title)

1914
27 June	Frank Moran, w pts 20r, Paris
	(World title)
15 Dec	Jack Murray, w ko r3, Buenos Aires

1915
5 Apl	Jess Willard, l ko r26, Havana
	(World title)

1916
10 Mar	Frank Crozier, w pts 10r, Madrid
10 July	Arthur Craven, w ko r1, Barcelona

1918
3 Apl	Blink McClosley, w pts 4r, Madrid

1919
12 Feb	Bill Flint, w ko r2, Madrid
7 Apl	Tom Cowler, d 10r, Mexico City
2 June	Tom Cowler, w ko r12, Mexico City
4 July	Paul Sampson, w ko r6, Mexico City
10 Aug	Marty Cutler, w ko r4, Mexico City
28 Sep	Bob Roper, w pts 10r, Mexico City

1920
18 Apl	Bob Wilson, w ko r3, Mexico City
17 May	George Roberts, w ko r3, Tia Juana

25 Nov   Frank Owens, w ko r6, Leavenworth
25 Nov   Top Johnson, w pts 5r, Leavenworth
30 Nov   George Owens, w ko r6, Leavenworth
1921
15 Apl   Jack Townsend, w ko r6, Leavenworth
1923
6 May   Farmer Lodge, w ko r4, Havana
20 May   Jack Thompson, no dec 15r, Havana
1924
22 Feb   Homer Smith, w pts 10r, Montreal
1926
2 May   Pat Lester, w pts 15r, Nogales, Mexico
30 May   Bob Lawson, w disq r8, Juarez, Mexico
1928
10 Apl   Bearcat Wright, l ko r2, Topeka
15 May   Bill Hartwell, l ko r6, Kansas City

Jack Dempsey
(William Harrison Dempsey)

Born 24 June 1895, Manassa, Colorado

1914
           Andy Molly, l pts 10r
17 Aug   Young Herman, d 6r, Ramona
1915
5 Apl   Jack Downey, l pts 4r, Salt Lake City
26 Apl   Anamas Campbell, w ko r3, Reno
13 June Johnny Sudenberg, w pts 10r, Tonopah
3 July   Johnny Sudenberg, d 10r, Goldfield
13 Dec   Jack Downey, d 4r, Salt Lake City
20 Dec   Two Round Gilhan, w ko r1, Salt Lake City
           Also in 1915, Dempsey scored knock-out victories
           over: Kid Hancock r1, Billy Murphy r1, Chief
           Gordon r6, Johnny Person r7, Joe Lions r9, Fred
           Woods r4, George Copelin r7, Andy Molloy r3,
           Battling Johnson r1, One-Punch Hancock r1; and
           drew over ten rounds with Andy Molloy.

1916
Jan   Boston Bearcat, w ko r1, Ogden
Feb   Johnny Sudenberg, w ko r2, Ely
21 Feb   Jack Downey, w ko r2, Salt Lake City
9 Mar   Cyril Kohn, w ko r4, Provo
8 Apl   Joe Bond, w pts 10r, Ely
3 May   Terry Keller, w pts 10r, Ogden
17 May   Dan Ketchell, w ko r3, Provo
May   George Christian, w ko r1, Price, Utah
June   Bob York, w ko r4, Price, Utah
24 June Andre Anderson, no dec 10r, New York
8 July   Wild Bert Kenny, no dec 10r, New York
14 July John L. Johnson, no dec 10r, New York
28 Sep   Young Hector, w ko r3, Salida
7 Oct   Terry Keller, w pts 10r, Ely
16 Oct   Dick Gilbert, w pts 10r, Salt Lake City
1917
13 Feb   Jim Flynn, l ko r1, Murray, Utah
28 Mar   Willie Meehan, l pts 4r, Oakland
11 Apl   Al Norton, d 4r, Oakland
21 May   Al Norton, d 4r, Oakland
25 July Willie Meehan, w pts 4r, San Francisco
1 Aug   Al Norton, w ko r1, San Francisco
10 Aug   Willie Meehan, d 4r, San Francisco
7 Sep   Willie Meehan, d 4r, San Francisco

19 Sep   Charlie Miller, w ko r1, Oakland
26 Sep   Bob McAllister, w pts 4r, Oakland
2 Oct   Gunboat Smith, w pts 4r, San Francisco
16 Oct   Gunboat Smith, no dec 4r, San Francisco
2 Nov   Carl Morris, w pts 4r, San Francisco
1918
24 Jan   Homer Smith, w ko r1, Racine
4 Feb   Carl Morris, w ko r1, Buffalo
14 Feb   Jim Flynn, w ko r1, Fort Sheridan
25 Feb   Bill Brennan, w ko r6, Milwaukee
16 Mar   Fred Saddy, w ko r1, Memphis
25 Mar   Tom Riley, w ko r1, Joplin
3 May   Billy Miske, no dec 10r, St Paul
22 May   Dan Ketchell, w ko r2, Excelsior
29 May   Arthur Pelky, w ko r1, Denver
1 July   Kid McCarthy, w ko r1, Tulsa
4 July   Bob Devere, w ko r1, Joplin
6 July   Porky Flynn, w ko r1, Atlanta
27 July Fred Fulton, w ko r1, Harrison
17 Aug   Terry Kellar, w ko r5, Dayton
13 Sep   Willie Meehan, l pts 4r, San Francisco
14 Sep   Jack Moran, w ko r1, Reno
6 Nov   Battling Levinsky, w ko r3, Philadelphia
18 Nov   Porky Flynn, w ko r1, Philadelphia
28 Nov   Billy Miske, no dec 6r, Philadelphia
16 Dec   Carl Morris, w ko r1, New Orleans
30 Dec   Gunboat Smith, w ko r2, Buffalo
1919
22 Jan   Big Jack Hickey, w ko r1, Harrisburg
23 Jan   Kid Harris, w ko r1, Reading
29 Jan   Kid Henry, w ko r1, Easton
13 Feb   Eddy Smith, w ko r1, Altoona
2 Apl   Tony Drake, w ko r1, New Haven
4 July   Jess Willard, w ko r3, Toledo
           (World title)
1920
6 Sep   Billy Miske, w ko r3, Benton Harbour
           (World title)
14 Dec   Bill Brennan, w ko r12, New York
           (World title)
1921
2 July   Georges Carpentier, w ko r4, Jersey City
           (World title)
1923
4 July   Tommy Gibbons, w pts 15r, Shelby
           (World title)
14 Sep   Luis Firpo, w ko r2, New York
           (World title)
1926
23 Sep   Gene Tunney, l pts 10r, Philadelphia
           (World title)
1927
21 July Jack Sharkey, w ko r7, New York
22 Sep   Gene Tunney, l pts 10r, Chicago
           (World title)

Joe Louis
(Joseph Louis Barrow)

Born 13 May 1914, Lafayette, Alabama

1934
4 July   Jack Kracken, w ko r1, Chicago
11 July Willie Davis, w ko r3, Chicago

29 July	Larry Udell, w ko r2, Chicago
13 Aug	Jack Kranz, w pts 8r, Chicago
27 Aug	Buck Everett, w ko r2, Chicago
11 Sep	Alex Burchuk, w ko r4, Detroit
25 Sep	Adolph Wiater, w pts 10r, Chicago
24 Oct	Art Sykes, w ko r8, Chicago
30 Oct	Jack O'Dowd, w ko r2, Detroit
14 Nov	Stanley Poreda, w ko r2, Chicago
30 Nov	Charley Massera, w ko r3, Chicago
14 Dec	Lee Ramage, w ko r8, Chicago

1935

4 Jan	Patsy Perroni, w pts 10r, Detroit
11 Jan	Hans Birkie, w ko r10, Pittsburgh
21 Feb	Lee Ramage, w ko r2, Los Angeles
8 Mar	Donald Barry, w ko r3, San Francisco
28 Mar	Natie Brown, w pts 10r, Detroit
12 Apl	Roy Lazer, w ko r3, Chicago
22 Apl	Biff Bentoff, w ko r2, Dayton
27 Apl	Roscoe Toles, w ko r6, Flint
3 May	Willie Davis, w ko r2, Peoria
7 May	Gene Stanton, w ko r3, Kalamazoo
25 June	Primo Carnera, w ko r6, New York City
7 Aug	King Levinsky, w ko r1, Chicago
24 Sep	Max Baer, w ko r4, New York City
13 Dec	Paolino Uzcudun, w ko r4, New York City

1936

17 Jan	Charley Retzlaff, w ko r1, Chicago
19 June	Max Schmeling, l ko r12, New York City
18 Aug	Jack Sharkey, w ko r3, New York City
22 Sep	Al Ettore, w ko r5, Philadelphia
9 Oct	Jorge Brescia, w ko r3, New York City
14 Dec	Eddie Simms, w ko r1, Cleveland

1937

11 Jan	Steve Ketchel, w ko r2, Buffalo
29 Jan	Bob Pastor, w pts 10r, New York City
17 Feb	Natie Brown, w ko r4, Kansas City
22 June	James J. Braddock, w ko r8, Chicago (World title)
30 Aug	Tommy Farr, w pts 15r, New York City (World title)

1938

23 Feb	Nathan Mann, w ko r3, New York City (World title)
1 Apl	Harry Thomas, w ko r5, Chicago (World title)
22 June	Max Schmeling, w ko r1, New York City (World title)

1939

25 Jan	John Henry Lewis, w ko r1, New York City (World title)
17 Apl	Jack Roper, w ko r1, Los Angeles (World title)
28 June	Tony Galento, w ko r4, New York City (World title)
20 Sep	Bob Pastor, w ko r11, Detroit (World title)

1940

9 Feb	Arturo Godoy, w pts 15r, New York City (World title)
29 May	Johnny Paychek, w ko r2, New York City (World title)
20 June	Arturo Godoy, w ko r8, New York City (World title)
16 Dec	Al McCoy, w ko r6, Boston (World title)

1941

31 Jan	Red Burman, w ko r5, New York City (World title)
17 Feb	Gus Dorazio, w ko r2, Philadelphia (World title)
21 Mar	Abe Simon, w ko r13, Detroit (World title)
8 Apl	Tony Musto, w ko r9, St Louis (World title)
23 May	Buddy Baer, w disq r7, Washington DC (World title)
18 June	Billy Conn, w ko r13, New York City (World title)
29 Sep	Lou Nova, w ko r6, New York City (World title)

1942

9 Jan	Buddy Baer, w ko r1, New York City (World title)
27 Mar	Abe Simon, w ko r6, New York City (World title)

1946

19 June	Billy Conn, w ko r8, New York City (World title)
18 Sep	Tami Mauriello, w ko r1, New York City (World title)

1947

5 Dec	Jersey Joe Walcott, w pts 15r, New York City (World title)

1948

25 June	Jersey Joe Walcott, w ko r11, New York City (World title)

1949

1 Mar	Announced retirement

1950

27 Sep	Ezzard Charles, l pts 15r, New York City (World title)
29 Nov	Cesar Brion, w pts 10r, Chicago

1951

3 Jan	Freddie Beshore, w ko r4, Detroit
7 Feb	Omelio Agramonte, w pts 10r, Miami
23 Feb	Andy Walker, w ko r10, San Francisco
2 May	Omelio Agramonte, w pts 10r, Detroit
15 June	Lee Savold, w ko r6, New York
1 Aug	Cesar Brion, w pts 10r, San Francisco
15 Aug	Jimmy Bivins, w pts 10r, Baltimore
26 Oct	Rocky Marciano, l ko r8, New York City

Rocky Marciano
(Rocco Francis Marchegiano)

Born 1 September 1923, Boston, Massachusetts

1947

17 Mar	Lee Epperson, w ko r3, Holyoke

1948

12 July	Harry Balzarian, w ko r1, Providence
19 July	John Edwards, w ko r1, Providence
9 Aug	Bobby Quinn, w ko r3, Providence
23 Aug	Eddie Ross, w ko r1, Providence
30 Aug	Jimmy Weeks, w ko r1, Providence
13 Sep	Jerry Jackson, w ko r1, Providence
20 Sep	Bill Hardeman, w ko r1, Providence
30 Sep	Gil Cardione, w ko r1, Washington DC

4 Oct	Bob Jefferson, w ko r2, Providence	
29 Nov	Patrick Connolly, w ko r1, Providence	
4 Dec	Gilley Ferron, w ko r2, Philadelphia	

1949

21 Mar	Johnny Pretzie, w ko r5, Providence
28 Mar	Artie Donater, w ko r1, Providence
11 Apl	James Walls, w ko r3, Providence
2 May	Jimmy Evans, w ko r3, Providence
23 May	Don Mogard, w pts 10r, Providence
18 July	Harry Haft, w ko r3, Providence
16 Aug	Pete Louthis, w ko r3, New Bedford
26 Sep	Tommy Di Giorgio, w ko r4, Providence
10 Oct	Ted Lowry, w pts 10r, Providence
7 Nov	Joe Dominic, w ko r2, Providence
2 Dec	Pat Richards, w ko r2, New York
19 Dec	Phil Muscato, w ko r5, Providence
30 Dec	Carmine Vingo, w ko r6, New York

1950

24 Mar	Roland LaStarza, w pts 10r, New York
5 June	Eldridge Eatman, w ko r3, Providence
10 July	Gino Buonvino, w ko r10, Boston
18 Sep	Johnny Shkor, w ko r6, Providence
13 Nov	Ted Lowry, w pts 10r, Providence
18 Dec	Bill Wilson, w ko r1, Providence

1951

29 Jan	Keene Simmons, w ko r8, Providence
20 Mar	Harold Mitchell, w ko r2, Hartford
26 Mar	Art Henri, w ko r9, Providence
30 Apl	Red Applegate, w pts 10r, Providence
12 July	Rex Layne, w ko r6, New York
27 Aug	Freddie Beshore, w ko r4, Boston
26 Oct	Joe Louis, w ko r8, New York

1952

13 Feb	Lee Savold, w ko r6, Philadelphia
21 Apl	Gino Buonvino, w ko r2, Providence
12 May	Bernie Reynolds, w ko r3, Providence
28 July	Harry Matthews, w ko r2, New York
23 Sep	Jersey Joe Walcott, w ko r13, Philadelphia (World title)

1953

15 May	Jersey Joe Walcott, w ko r1, Chicago (World title)
24 Sep	Roland LaStarza, w ko r11, New York (World title)

1954

17 June	Ezzard Charles, w pts 15r, New York (World title)
17 Sep	Ezzard Charles, w ko r8, New York (World title)

1955

16 May	Don Cockell, w ko r9, San Francisco (World title)
21 Sep	Archie Moore, w ko r9, New York (World title)

Muhammad Ali
(Cassius Clay)

Born 17 January 1942, Louisville, Kentucky

1960

29 Oct	Tunney Hunsaker, w pts 6r, Louisville
27 Dec	Herb Siler, w ko r4, Miami Beach

1961

17 Jan	Tony Esperti, w ko r3, Miami Beach
7 Feb	Jim Robinson, w ko r1, Miami Beach
21 Feb	Donnie Fleeman, w ko r7, Miami Beach
19 Apl	Lamar Clark, w ko r2, Louisville
26 June	Duke Sabedong, w pts 10r, Las Vegas
22 July	Alonzo Johnson, w pts 10r, Louisville
7 Oct	Alex Miteff, w ko r6, Louisville
29 Nov	Willi Besmanoff, w ko r7, Louisville

1962

10 Feb	Sonny Banks, w ko r4, New York
28 Feb	Don Warmer, w ko r4, Miami Beach
23 Apl	George Logan, w ko r4, Los Angeles
19 May	Billy Daniels, w ko r7, New York
20 July	Alejandro Lavorante, w ko r5, Los Angeles
15 Nov	Archie Moore, w ko r4, Los Angeles

1963

24 Jan	Charlie Powell, w ko r3, Pittsburgh
13 Mar	Doug Jones, w pts 10r, New York
8 June	Henry Cooper, w rsf r5, London

1964

25 Feb	Sonny Liston, w rtd r6, Miami Beach (World title)

1965

25 May	Sonny Liston, w ko r1, Lewiston (World title)
22 Nov	Floyd Patterson, w ko r12, Las Vegas (World title)

1966

29 Mar	George Chuvalo, w pts 15r, Toronto (World title)
21 May	Henry Cooper, w rsf r6, London (World title)
6 Aug	Brian London, w ko r3, London (World title)
10 Sep	Karl Mildenberger, w ko r12, Frankfurt (World title)
14 Nov	Cleveland Williams, w ko r3, Houston (World title)

1967

6 Feb	Ernie Terrell, w pts 15r, Houston (World title)
22 Mar	Zora Folley, w ko r7, New York City (World title)
28 Apl	Stripped of title

1970

26 Oct	Jerry Quarry, w ko r3, Atlanta
7 Dec	Oscar Bonavena, w ko r15, New York City

1971

8 Mar	Joe Frazier, l pts 15r, New York City (World title)
26 July	Jimmy Ellis, w ko r12, Houston
17 Nov	Buster Mathis, w pts 12r, Houston
26 Dec	Jurgen Blin, w ko r7, Zurich

1972

1 Apl	Mac Foster, w pts 15r, Tokyo
1 May	George Chuvalo, w pts 12r, Vancouver
27 June	Jerry Quarry, w ko r7, Las Vegas
19 July	Al Lewis, w ko r11, Dublin
20 Sep	Floyd Patterson, w ko r7, New York City
21 Nov	Bob Foster, w ko r8, Stateline

1973

14 Feb	Joe Bugner, w pts 12r, Las Vegas
31 Mar	Ken Norton, l pts 12r, San Diego
10 Sep	Ken Norton, w pts 12r, Inglewood
20 Oct	Rudi Lubbers, w pts 12r, Jakarta

1974

| 28 Jan | Joe Frazier, w pts 12r, New York City |
| 30 Oct | George Foreman, w ko r8, Kinshasa (World title) |

1975

24 Mar	Chuck Wepner, w rsf r15, Cleveland (World title)
16 May	Ron Lyle, w rsf r11, Las Vegas (World title)
1 July	Joe Bugner, w pts 15r, Kuala Lumpur (World title)
1 Oct	Joe Frazier, w rtd r14, Manila (World title)

1976

20 Feb	Jean-Pierre Coopman, w ko r5, San Juan (World title)
30 Apl	Jimmy Young, w pts 15r, Landover (World title)
25 May	Richard Dunn, w rsf r5, Munich (World title)
28 Sep	Ken Norton, w pts 15r, New York City (World title)

1977

| 16 May | Alfredo Evangelista, w pts 15r, Maryland (World title) |
| 29 Sep | Earnie Shavers, w pts 15r, New York City (World title) |

1978

| 22 Feb | Leon Spinks, l pts 15r, Las Vegas (World title) |

Henry Cooper

Born 3 May 1934, Bellingham, London

1954

14 Sep	Harry Painter, w ko r1, London
19 Oct	Dinny Powell, w rsf, r4, London
23 Nov	Eddie Keith, w rsf r1, London
7 Dec	Denny Ball, w ko r3, London

1955

27 Jan	Colin Strauch, w rsf r1, London
8 Feb	Cliff Purnell, w pts 6r, London
8 Mar	Hugh Ferns, w disq r12, London
19 Mar	Joe Crickmar, w rtd r5, London
18 Apl	Joe Bygraves, w pts 8r, London
26 Apl	Uber Bacilieri, l rsf r2, London
6 June	Ron Harman, w rsf r7, Nottingham
13 Sep	Uber Bacilieri, w ko r7, London
15 Nov	Joe Erskine, l pts 10r, London

1956

28 Feb	Maurice Mols, w rsf r4, London
1 May	Brian London, w rsf r1, London
26 June	Giannino Luise, w rsf r7, London
7 Sep	Peter Bates, l rtd r5, Manchester

1957

19 Feb	Joe Bygraves, l ko r9, London (Empire title)
19 May	Ingemar Johansson, l ko r5, Stockholm (European title)
17 Sep	Joe Erskine, l pts 15r, London
16 Nov	Hans Kalbfell, w pts 10r, Dortmund

1958

| 1 Jan | Heinz Neuhaus, d 10r, Dortmund |

19 Apl	Erich Schoeppner, l disq r6, Frankfurt
3 Sep	Dick Richardson, w rsf r5, Porthcawl
14 Oct	Zora Folley, w pts 10r, London

1959

12 Jan	Brian London, w pts 15r, London (British and Empire titles)
26 Aug	Gawie de Klerk, w rsf r5, Porthcawl (Empire title)
17 Nov	Joe Erskine, w rsf r12, London (British and Empire titles)

1960

| 13 Sep | Roy Harris, w pts 10r, London |
| 6 Dec | Alex Miteff, w pts 10r, London |

1961

| 21 Mar | Joe Erskine, w rtd r5, London (British and Empire titles) |
| 5 Dec | Zora Folley, l ko r2, London |

1962

23 Jan	Tony Hughes, w rtd r5, London
26 Feb	Wayne Bethea, w pts 10r, Manchester
2 Apl	Joe Erskine, w rsf r9, Nottingham (British and Empire titles)

1963

| 26 Mar | Dick Richardson, w ko r5, London (British and Empire titles) |
| 18 June | Cassius Clay (Muhammad Ali), l rsf r5, London |

1964

| 24 Feb | Brian London, w pts 15r, Manchester (Empire and European titles) |
| 16 Nov | Roger Rischer, l pts 10r, London |

1965

12 Jan	Dick Wipperman, w rsf r5, London
20 Apl	Chip Johnson, w ko r1, Wolverhampton
15 June	Johnny Prescott, w rtd r10, Birmingham (British and Empire titles)
19 Oct	Amos Johnson, l pts 10r, London

1966

25 Jan	Hubert Hilton, w rsf r2, London
16 Feb	Jefferson Davis, w ko r1, Wolverhampton
21 May	Muhammad Ali, l rsf r6, London (World title)
20 Sep	Floyd Patterson, l ko r4, London

1967

17 Apl	Boston Jacobs, w pts 10r, Leicester
13 June	Jack Bodell, w rsf r2, Wolverhampton (British and Empire titles)
7 Nov	Billy Walker, w rsf r6, London (British and Empire titles)

1968

| 18 Sep | Karl Mildenberger, w disq r8, London (European title) |

1969

| 13 Mar | Piero Tomasoni, w ko r5, Rome (European title) |

1970

| 24 Mar | Jack Bodell, w pts 15r, London (British and Commonwealth titles) |
| 10 Nov | José Urtain, w rsf r9, London (European title) |

1971

| 16 Mar | Joe Bugner, l pts 15r, London (British, European and Commonwealth titles) |

Index

Page numbers in italics refer to illustrations

Acknowledgements

The photographs in this publication are from the Gilbert Odd Collection with the exception of the following:
Associated Press Ltd., London 62 bottom, 63 top, 81 bottom, 94 top, 146–147; British Broadcasting Corporation, London 15; Keystone Press Agency Ltd., London 10; Popperfoto, London 6–7, 45 top, 46 top, 78–79, 82 top, 82 bottom left, 83 top, 83 bottom left, 83 bottom right, 84 bottom left, 84–85 top and title page, 85 bottom, 88 bottom, 89 top, 89 bottom, 90 centre, 90 bottom, 91 top, 91 bottom, 92 top, 92 bottom, 93 top, 94 bottom, 96 bottom, 97 top, 97 bottom, 98 top, 98 bottom, 99 top, 99 bottom, 100 top, 100 bottom, 101 top, 101 bottom, 138–139, 143 top, 143 bottom and half title page, 144 top, 144 bottom, 145 top, 147 top right, 147 bottom right, 148–149, 149 right, 150, 151, 152, 153, 157 top, 158 top, 158 bottom, 159 top, 159 bottom, 161 top, 161 bottom, 162 top, 162 bottom, 164, 165, 166, 167, 168–169; Sport and General, London 80 top; Syndication International, London 80 bottom; Topix, London 89 centre.

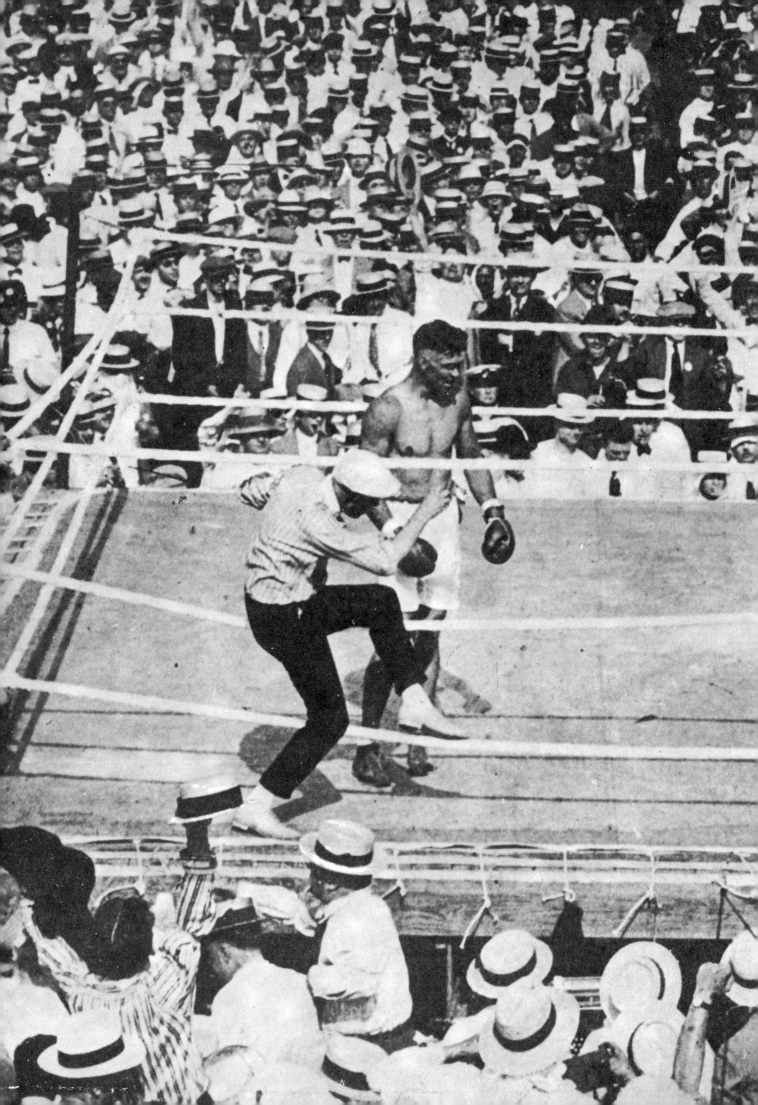